Reviews

"Bruce Hartford is a national treasure. This captivating people's history draws on firsthand witness that he has devoted a lifetime to gather and preserve. It brings alive the everyday heroes of Selma, whose messy, deep, authentic struggle opened stubborn gates to freedom for the whole country only fifty years ago."

— Taylor Branch, Pulitzer-Prize winning author of *America in the King Years*.

"Hartford's vivid depiction of the voting rights struggle in Selma, Alabama brings the reader into the thick of the freedom movement. One sees first through eight year old Rachel West's eyes — of the rope, the troopers, the singing — as she stood vigil in the rain. Then through the eyes of President Johnson, who faced down fellow white southern lawmakers by embracing the movement's anthem, "We Shall Overcome." And yet again, through the eyes of grassroots civil rights workers who heard Johnson's speech and felt irate at the president's burning hypocrisy. It is only by such work as Hartford's — that of weaving together such "thick memories" in the struggle — that the nation will be able to internalize the hard won lessons the movement offers. This book serves as essential witness to the most basic building block of democratic practice, 'One Person, One Vote.' "

— Wesley Hogan, Director of Center for Documentary Studies, Duke University

"This book is a Movement Diary of the voting rights struggles in Selma, Alabama in the early 1960s. It chronicles the day to-day epic battles that occurred between the irresistible forces (the black people of Alabama, Dallas County Voter League, SNCC, and SCLC) and the once considered immovable objects (segregation and the denial of the right to vote). The book also provides great insights into the strategies and tactics of civil leaders — Martin Luther King, Jr., John Lewis, Hosea Williams, and Silas Norman — as they battled the barriers to voting rights. The campaign for voting rights in Selma, Alabama resulted in the Voting Rights Act of 1965."

— Courtland Cox, President SNCC Legacy Project

"Nothing exists of this depth. No historian of the Freedom Movement and certainly no scholar studying the Selma voting rights movement and the Selma to Montgomery march will be able to do so without using this book. It is invaluable and typical of what is found on the Civil Rights Movement veterans' site."

— Charlie Cobb, author of *This Nonviolent Stuff'll Get You Killed*, Basic Books

"No one has delved into this aspect of the movement in as much depth from a witness/participant perspective. Through his dedication to managing the Civil Rights Veterans' website: www.crmvet.org, Bruce Hartford has amassed an invaluable collection of original documents of the civil rights movement and witness/participant interviews. His analysis contains keen insights, behind the scenes perspectives, and the healthy skepticism of a lay historian who checks his facts. A definite read for anyone who cares about what really happened in Selma.

—Maria Gitin, *This Bright Light of Ours: Stories from the Voting Rights Fight*, University of Alabama Press

"Bruce Hartford's engaging account of the 1965 Selma campaign combines a helpful introduction to the Civil Rights Movement and key organizations, with a compelling, detailed account of events in Selma. He brings to life the tedium and danger of the day in, day out organizing of SNCC field secretaries Bernard and Colia Lafayette working with stalwart local activists before moving on to the dramatic events that culminated in the Selma to Montgomery March and the passage of the landmark Voting Rights Act of 1965. As we approach the 50th anniversary of these events in the context of new challenges to minority voting rights, this history is particularly important. Hartford's vivid, accessible account is a wonderful resource and one that will be useful and appealing to newcomers and specialists alike.

— Emilye Crosby, professor of history at State University of New York, Geneseo, author of *A Little Taste of Freedom*, editor of *Civil Rights History from the Ground Up*.

"Bruce Hartford has created a brilliant piece about the voting rights struggle in Selma in 1965, covering what was going on before, during, and after the Selma March. This is a definitive work: well written, detailed but easily read, well conceived, compact, moving, and accessible. I could not stop reading once I began. This material is for those who know only the highlights, are versed in these events but seek more, and for those who were there but want to revisit what was going on around them. Hartford is the webmaster of www.crmvet.org, a major resource of the human rights struggle in the South."

— Don Jelinek, SNCC member and civil rights lawyer, author of the forthcoming, *White Lawyer, Black Power: Civil Rights Lawyering during the Black Power Era in Mississippi and Alabama*.

The Selma Voting Rights Struggle & the March to Montgomery

Bruce Hartford

Westwind Writers

The Selma Voting Rights Struggle & March to Montgomery
Bruce Hartford / Author
Copyright © 2014. All rights reserved.
ISBN 978-0-9778000-2-5
Freedom Now! Series
Published by Westwind Writers
2301 Harrison St. #205
San Francisco, CA 94110
wwwriters.com
bruceh@wwwriters.com

Dedication

For the winter soldiers of the Freedom Movement

Acknowledgements

The book could not have been written without the input, commentary, discussions, debates, suggestions, and support of Bay Area Veterans of the Civil Rights Movement — Chude Pam Parker Allen, Hardy Frye, Miriam Glickman, Phil Hutchings, Don Jelinek, Betita Martinez, Mike Miller, Wazir Peacock, Jimmy Rogers, and Jean Wiley.

Nor could it have been created without the book design skills and doggedly determined editing of Bonnie Britt.

More information on the *Selma Voting Rights Struggle and the March to Montgomery* is on the Civil Rights Movement Veterans website: crmvet.org

Cover photo: © Matt Herron, 1965. (Take Stock: Images of Change: www.takestockphotos.com/)

Contents

Dedication	vii
Acknowledgements	viii
Introduction	

chapter 1
The Struggle in Selma: 1963–1964 9

    Selma — Breaking the Grip of Fear, 1963 13
    Freedom Day in Selma, 1963 18
    The Selma Injunction, 1964 23

chapter 2
Selma Voting Rights Campaign of 1965 27

    The Situation 27
    The Alabama Project 29
    SCLC and SNCC 33
    Selma on the Eve 36
    Breaking the Selma Injunction 39
    Marching to the Courthouse 41
    The Teachers March 45
    Annie Cooper and Sheriff Clark 49
    Letter from a Selma Jail 52
    Malcolm X Speaks in Selma 57
    Bound in Jail 58
    Clubs and Cattle Prods 60
    Holding On and Pushing Forward 62

Contents

The Shooting of Jimmy Lee Jackson	68
Tension Escalates	72

chapter 3
The March to Montgomery — 79

March 7, "Bloody Sunday"	79
Call...	87
Monday, March 8	92
... and Response	95
Tuesday, March 9	98
Judge Johnson's Injunction	99
Turnaround Tuesday	102
Savage Assault on Unitarian Ministers	108
Meetings and Decisions	110
Wednesday, March 10	110
"The Berlin Wall"	112
Hearing Before Federal Judge Johnson	115
Students March in Montgomery	117
Thursday, March 11	122
Confrontation at Dexter Church	123
Death of Rev. Reeb	125
Friday, March 12 – Sunday, March 14	126
Monday, March 15	129
Protests and Police Violence Continue	131
Reeb Memorial March in Selma	132
President Johnson: "We Shall Overcome"	135
Tuesday, March 16	137

Contents

Brutal Attack in Montgomery	137
Wednesday, March 17	140
Mass March to Montgomery Courthouse	141
Judge Johnson Finally Rules	142
March 18–20, Organizing the March	143
March 21–24, Marching to Montgomery	148
March 25, Marching on the Capitol	157

chapter 4
Aftermath — 165

Murder and Character Assassination of Viola Liuzzo	167

Appendix — 175
Voting Rights and So-Called "Literacy Tests" — 175

Registering to Vote in Alabama	176
Alabama Voter Application	178
Alabama Literacy Test	182
"Part A"	182
"Part B"	183
"Part C"	184

Quotation Sources — 189
About the Author — 191

Introduction

The Southern Freedom Movement of the 1950s and 1960s addressed two main issues — segregation and voting rights. In early 1965, the long campaign to win Black voting rights in the South climaxes with the Selma Voting Rights Campaign and the March to Montgomery. Sometimes referred to as America's "Second Reconstruction," this fight for Black voting rights has a long and deep history leading up to the Selma campaign.

1864–1870: The 13th, 14th & 15th Amendments end slavery and grant citizenship and voting rights to Blacks.

1866–1964: Subversion of the 14th & 15th Amendments. Whites in the South (and elsewhere) use violence, economic terrorism, and restrictive legislation to subvert the amendments. "Black Codes" restrict Afro-American's property, business, travel, voting, and other citizenship rights. "Jim Crow" segregation laws mandate racial separation in public accommodations, education, marriage, housing, medical care, employment and other phases of life. Federal efforts to enforce Black rights are half-hearted and of limited effect.

1876–1877: "Compromise" of 1877 eliminates federal protection of Blacks. In the disputed presidential election of 1876, Samuel Tilden, a Democrat, wins the popular vote. But vote counts are disputed in Florida and two other southern states leaving the Electoral College results unresolved. In return for Democrats acceding to his election, Rutherford Hayes, the Republican, agrees to end Reconstruction and U.S. military occupation of the South.

1877: Reconstruction ends. With troops no longer protecting Blacks, a wave of racist violence washes across the South. Federal officials abandon all pretense of defending Black rights. Black attempts to assert or defend their human and civil rights are crushed by white violence, economic terrorism, and state repression. Though Black resistance to white supremacy in the South is driven underground, it is not extinguished — for three generations southern Blacks covertly resist where they can and endure what they must.

1896: In Plessy v Ferguson, the Supreme Court rules that racial segregation laws are constitutional. With the "Jim Crow" system ratified and condoned by the Supreme Court, a complex web of laws, customs, and procedures mandating, establishing, and maintaining racial discrimination spread across the nation.

1909: The National Association for the Advancement of Colored People (NAACP) is founded to secure the rights guaranteed in the 13th, 14th, and 15th amendments, ensure the rights of all persons regardless of race or color, and to eliminate racial hatred and discrimination. Within a short time it has active (but often covert) chapters throughout the South.

1918: Black veterans of World War I (*"the war to make the world safe for democracy"*) return home and attempt to register to vote. In the South, their efforts are crushed by violence, state repression, and economic terrorism.

1945: Black veterans of World War II fight for democracy at home. As with WWI, when Black veterans of the Second World War (the *"fight for the Four Freedoms"*) return home they attempt to register as voters. Again, their efforts are crushed by violence, state repression, and economic terrorism.

1951: Murder of Harry & Harriet Moore. Florida voter registration activists and NAACP leaders Harry & Harriet Moore are burned to death when the KKK bombs their home near Titusville.

Introduction

1954: Citizenship Schools. With the assistance of the Highlander Center, Esau Jenkins and Septima Clark begin organizing Citizenship Schools in the South. Under the innocuous cover of adult-literacy classes, the schools begin teaching democracy, civil rights, community leadership, organizing, practical politics, and the strategies and tactics of nonviolent resistance. When the Highlander Center comes under attack by the state of Tennessee, the Southern Christian Leadership Conference (SCLC) agrees to sustain and expand the program.

1955: Murder of Rev. George Wesley Lee. NAACP leader and voter registration activist Rev. George Wesley Lee is shot to death on a Mississippi road. No one is ever arrested for this murder. Witnesses describe how whites in another vehicle fire a shotgun into Lee's car. The local sheriff declares his murder to be "death by unknown cause," and he claims that the lead shotgun pellets in Lee's face are "dental fillings."

1957–1961: Tuskegee gerrymander and boycott. When a number of Blacks manage to become registered voters in Tuskegee Alabama, the Alabama legislature redraws the Tuskegee town boundaries from a simple square to a twisted, 27-sided, "gerrymandered" shape that excludes Tuskegee Institute and all but a handful of Black voters. Blacks launch an economic boycott of the white-owned stores in Tuskegee. The boycott lasts four years, with devastating economic consequences for the white merchants who would rather go out of business than allow Blacks to vote. The boycott ends in 1961 when the U.S. Supreme Court rules that gerrymandered districts designed to restrict Blacks from voting are unconstitutional. The old town boundaries are restored.

1959–1965: Fayette County Tent City. When Blacks in Fayette and Haywood counties in Tennessee begin registering to vote in significant numbers, the White Citizens Council distributes lists of Black voters to merchants who refuse to sell them the necessities of life (food, clothing, gasoline, etc). White doctors withold medical treatment, wholesalers and distributors refuse to supply Black-owned stores, and insurance companies cancel policies. To drive Black voters out of the two counties, white landowners evict more than 400 Black sharecroppers and bankers foreclose on home mortgages. Many of the dispossessed move into a tent encampment — known as "Freedom Village" or "Tent City." Says Georgia Mae Turner, *"They say if you register, you going to have a hard time. Well, I had a hard time before I registered. Hard times — you could have named me 'Georgia Mae Hard Times.' The reason I registered, because I want to be a citizen. ... I registered so that my children could get their freedom."*

1961: McComb MS voter registration struggle. In August of 1961, the Student Nonviolent Coordinating Committee (SNCC, pronounced "Snick") begins a voter registration project in McComb Mississippi that quickly expands to surrounding Pike, Amite, and Walthall counties. White reaction is immediate and violent. SNCC workers are assaulted, beaten, and arrested on trumped-up charges. Blacks who try to register are threatened, student supporters are arrested and expelled. Herbert Lee a 42-year old Black farmer attempts to register to vote in Amite County. He is murdered by State Representative E.H. Hurst who is quickly released after a coroners jury declares the killing a "justifiable homicide." More than 100 students and most of the SNCC staff are arrested for nonviolently marching in protest. Bail for the SNCC workers is set at $14,000 each (equal to $107,000 in 2012 dollars). Unable to raise such a huge amount, they languish in prison. Violence and state repression manage to temporarily suppress the voter campaign in McComb.

1962: Struggling for the vote in Greenwood MS. When finally released from jail, the SNCC organizers carry their voter-registration campaign into the Mississippi Delta, centered on the small town of Greenwood. Fear is pervasive among Greenwood Blacks. Fear of being fired. Fear of being evicted. Fear of beatings, bombings, and murder. But gradually, week by week, month

Introduction

by month, as the young SNCC "field secretaries" persevere, trust is built and their courage inspires first the young students and then their parents. A church dares to open its doors for a voter registration meeting. The community begins coming together. A mob of white racists attack the SNCC office, and the SNCC organizers barely escape over the roof tops, but they carry on. Slowly, one by one, two by two, a trickle of Leflore County Blacks begin to make the dangerous journey down to the courthouse to try to register to vote. But in the first six months, only five Blacks, of the dozens who try, are actually registered.

The White Citizens Council strikes back. For sharecroppers and farm laborers in the Delta, winter is the lean time, the hard time. One-third of the population struggles to survive on an annual income of less than $500 per year (equal to $3800 in 2012). With no work and nothing to eat, they rely on federal surplus food commodities for survival. As winter closes in, the Council has the County Board of Supervisors stop distributing federal food aid to 22,000 Leflore County citizens — most of them Black. SNCC leader Bob Moses later writes to a northern supporter:

> We do need the actual food. ... Just this afternoon, I was sitting reading, having finished a bowl of stew, and a silent hand reached over from behind, its owner mumbling some words of apology and stumbling up with a neckbone from the plate under the bowl, one which I had discarded, which had some meat on it. The hand was back again, five seconds later, groping for the potatoe I had left in the bowl. I never saw the face. I didn't look. The hand was dark, a man's hand, dry and wind-cracked, from the cotton chopping and cotton picking. — Bob Moses. [5]

Meanwhile, another SNCC voter-registration project takes root in Southwest Georgia. Centered on the city of Albany, it slowly expands into the surrounding plantation counties — Sumter, "Terrible Terell," and "Bad Baker" where white supremacy is ruthlessly maintained with club, jail, gun, and bomb. And at the turning of the year, two courageous SNCC organizers — Bernard and Colia Lidell Lafayette — quietly slip into Selma, Alabama, a town notorious for brutal racism, violence, and repression.

1963: One man, one vote. Federal efforts to enforce voting rights remain reluctant and ineffectual. They focus on "equal application of the law." State laws require that prospective voters pass complex and arcane literacy tests, and the segregated school systems systematically deny an adequate education to the overwhelming majority of Blacks. If equal application of the law ever actually occurred, it would simply result in disenfranchisement of a good many illiterate whites, and just a small increase in the number of Black voters. In response, SNCC, followed by Congress of Racial Equality (CORE) and SCLC, take the radical step of challenging the entire concept of voter "qualification." Voting is not about academic achievement, it's about political power and electing the officials who make and enforce the laws that everyone must obey. All citizens should have a right to vote regardless of their education — a position they sum up with the slogan: *"One Man, One Vote."*

1963: Freedom ballot in Mississippi. All the candidates in the Mississippi general election of November 1963 are segregationists. Even if Blacks could vote, they have no one to vote for. The Movement organizes an unofficial "Freedom Ballot" with an integrated slate of pro-freedom candidates. Based on the "One Man, One Vote" principle, all adult citizens are eligible to vote regardless of whether they are registered. The Freedom Ballot is designed to show that Blacks in large numbers want to vote but are denied the right to do so, and that the white segregationists elected to office do not represent Mississippi Blacks. Recognizing a potent protest when they see one, the white power structure uses violence, arrests, and economic retaliation to suppress the Freedom Vote even though it's just a mock ballot with no legal validity. But their efforts fail. In churches and other venues, Freedom Voting takes place from Friday, November 1st

Introduction

to Tuesday the 5th, with records kept so that no one can vote more than once. More than 80,000 people — four times the total number of Blacks registered to vote — defy the cops, the Klan, and the Citizens Council to mark Freedom Ballots.

1964: Freedom Summer. After years of struggle, years of hard dangerous work, years of beatings, jailings, bombings, and murders only a handful of new Black voters have been added to the voting rolls in Mississippi. In a bold move, the Movement issues a call for supporters to spend a "Freedom Summer" in the state. More than a thousand respond — most of them college students, most of them white, but also including lawyers, clergy, and medical professionals. More than 17,000 Blacks defiantly line up at county courthouses to register — but only 1600 (just 9% of those who apply) are allowed to become voters.

And the human cost is staggering: At least seven people (5 Black, 2 white) are murdered by white racists. There are 35 shootings with four people critically wounded. At least 80 people are beaten by white mobs or police, more than 1,000 are arrested on various trumped-up charges. Some 37 Black churches and 30 Black homes or businesses are burned or bombed. And an unknown number of Blacks are fired from their jobs or evicted from their homes for attempting to register to vote or for otherwise supporting the Freedom Movement.

Though few voters are added to the rolls, Freedom Summer begins to break the reign of fear and isolation that has oppressed Mississippi Blacks for generations. As one volunteer deep in the Delta writes, *"In Panola County now the Negro citizens look with pride at their names in the "Panolian" [list of voter applicants], they point out the names of friends and neighbors and hurry to the courthouse to be enlisted on the honor roll."*

1960–1965: Fighting for the vote across the South. Though these examples of Black voter registration efforts and white resistance are drawn mainly from the struggle in Mississippi, similar events are taking place across the South from Texas to the Eastern

Shore of Maryland. In Loiusiana, CORE spearheads campaigns across the state in the face of fierce Klan opposition. In Southwest Georgia, four freedom workers face the death penalty on charges of "Seditious Conspiracy," an old slavery-era law enacted to suppress Black resistance to white rule. In North and South Carolina, NAACP, CORE, and Southern Conference Education Fund (SCEF) organizers confront both violence and economic terrorism in the voting rights fight. In town after town, students too young to vote march for equal rights in support of their parents' efforts. After six weeks in a Georgia jail without bail or trial, 13- year old Gloria Breedlove tells a journalist: *"The minute I became a freedom rider, I was choosing to abandon my jump rope and be a soldier for freedom."*

chapter 1

The Struggle in Selma: 1963–1964

Geologically, the "Black Belt" is a swath of rich dark soil that runs from Virginia down through the Carolinas, Georgia, Alabama, over to the Mississippi Delta region and portions of Arkansas, Tennessee, and Louisiana. Historically, the fertile earth of this multi-state Black Belt region was the center of large-scale, labor-intensive, plantation-style agriculture, primarily cotton and tobacco. Before the Civil War, those plantations were worked by Black slaves, and afterward by Black and white sharecroppers and tenant farmers.

In the 1960s, either Blacks still comprise a majority or close to a majority of most Black Belt county populations, and the term "Black Belt" is often used to refer to those demographics rather than the soil. In rural Black Belt counties, economic exploitation, white supremacy, and state-repression are both brutal and intense.

Blacks endure grinding poverty, inadequate housing and healthcare, "share-cropper education," and an absence of the civil and human rights that white Americans take for granted. Selma, Alabama is the seat of Dallas County.

The Selma Voting Rights Struggle

Alabama Black Belt

Selma is also the unofficial economic, political, and cultural capitol of the western portion of Alabama's Black Belt. The county is 57% Black in 1961, but of the 15,000 Afro-Americans old enough to vote only 130 — less than 1% — are registered — and some of those few actually live and work elsewhere. Selma is also the unofficial economic, political, and cultural capitol of the western portion of Alabama's Black Belt. The county is 57% Black in 1961, but of the 15,000 Afro-Americans old enough to vote only 130 — less than 1% — are registered — and some of those few actually live and work elsewhere. More than 80% of

Selma: 1963–1964

Dallas County Blacks live below the poverty line. Most of them work as sharecroppers, farm hands, maids, janitors, and day-laborers. Only 5% of Dallas County Blacks have a high school diploma, and more than 60% never had the chance to go to high School at all because neither Alabama nor the local school board see any need to educate the "hewers of wood and drawers of water." By contrast, 81% of Dallas County whites live above the poverty line and 90% have at least a high School education.

In the rural counties surrounding Selma, the Black majorities are even larger — over 80% in some cases — and in many of them, not a single Afro-American is registered. Adjacent Wilcox County is 78% Black and has not had an Afro voter since the end of Reconstruction. Neither has next door Lowndes County, which is over 81% Black.

Judge James Hare dominates Dallas County politics, and the county is sometimes referred to as a "political plantation," with Judge Hare as master and Sheriff Jim Clark as whip-cracking overseer. Judge Hare is a self-proclaimed "expert" on racial eugenics. He asserts that the Blacks living in Selma are descended from Ibo and Angolan slaves who (in his publicly stated opinion) are genetically incapable of having an IQ of higher 65. Clark is a brutal, hard-core racist, whose strategy for maintaining rigid segregation is to violently beat down and arrest anyone who dares question the established order. Using bribery, intimidation, and blackmail, Clark has built a network of Black snitches who inform on their neighbors.

In addition to his paid deputies, Clark relies on his Sheriff's posse of more than two hundred armed volunteers — some of them members or supporters of racist organizations such as the Ku Klux Klan. Possemen wear cheap badges issued by Clark, construction helmets, and khaki work clothes. They are armed with shotguns, pistols, and a variety of hardwood clubs including ax-handles. Originally formed after World War II to oppose labor unions, the posse's current mission is to defend white supremacy and suppress all forms of Black protest. The posse isn't limited to just Dallas County; Clark sends them on missions far and wide.

The Selma Voting Rights Struggle

In 1961, some were part of the mob that beat the Freedom Riders in Montgomery, others rushed to join the massive violence in Oxford, Mississippi when James Meredith integrated 'Ole Miss' in 1962, and Bull Connor called them in to help crack the heads of student protesters during the Birmingham Campaign of 1963.

Supporting Hare and Clark is Selma's powerful White Citizens Council composed of bankers, businessmen, politicians, landlords, clergy, and other pillars of the community. The Council stands ever vigilant against any attempt to undermine the "Southern way of life," which they defend with economic terrorism — firings, evictions, foreclosures, blacklists, and business boycotts. Together, Judge Hare, Sheriff Clark, the posse, the Citizens Council, and the snitches create an interlocking reign of economic, judicial, and violent terror that imprison Dallas County Blacks in an iron grip of fear.

But violence, jail, and economic terrorism cannot entirely suppress the spirit of resistance in Selma.

> Selma was a different place [from the Mississippi Delta]. Very different. No less oppressive or brutal, but so very different. For one thing, I really liked that African community. See, if I say that racism in Selma was as ruthless, the segregation as complete as any I yet seen, but that the black community was more together — psychologically and culturally a proud community — than many I'd seen, it must certainly sound like a contradiction. But that was the Lord's truth. Could be that the strength was a consequence of the severity of the racism, or that the oppression was so severe because of the cultural strength of the Africans. Or both? Whatever the case, many movement people have said that Selma people were the "most African" blacks in the South. I could see exactly what they meant. The community was poor and economically oppressed, true. But it was also self-contained and self-sufficient with businesses (small but our own) and black professionals, and strong in black religion and

culture, with even two tiny church-affiliated colleges, Lutheran College and Selma University. — Kwame Ture (Stokely Carmichael). [1]

A few courageous souls keep the hope of freedom alive in Selma, Alabama. The Boynton family — Sam, Amelia, and their son Bruce — are not intimidated. While a student at Howard Law School, Bruce Boynton is arrested for using a white-only lunch counter at the Trailways bus station in Richmond VA. He files *Boynton v. Virginia,* the landmark Supreme Court case that overturns segregation in interstate travel and forms the legal basis for the Freedom Rides in 1961.

After the Supreme Court's 1954 *Brown v Board of Education* school desegregation ruling and the 1955–56 Montgomery Bus Boycott, the Alabama Attorney General retaliates against the NAACP by mounting a legal attack that cripples the organization and drives it underground for years. The Boyntons, Rev. L.L. Anderson of Tabernacle Baptist Church, J.L. Chestnut (Selma's first Black attorney), dental technician and SCLC Citizenship School teacher Marie Foster, educator James Gildersleeve, school teacher Margaret Moore, and others respond by reviving the old Dallas County Voter's League (DCVL) of which Sam is chosen president. Against the entrenched power of Hare, Clark, and the Citizens Council they make little progress as the fifties end and the sixties begin, but they refuse to surrender to despair or apathy.

Selma — Breaking the Grip of Fear, 1963

At the turning of the year, in January 1963, Bernard and Colia Lafayette arrive in Selma, Alabama. They are a pair of newly-wed organizers working for the Student Nonviolent Coordinating Committee (SNCC). Bernard is a veteran leader of the Nashville Student Movement, a Freedom Rider, and a Mississippi voter registration worker. Colia Lidell Lafayette is a student activist and protest leader from Tougaloo College in Mississippi, founder and president of the NAACP's North

The Selma Voting Rights Struggle

Jackson Youth Council, and former assistant to Medgar Evers. Their mission is to register voters and build the Freedom Movement in the Black Belt of Alabama.

They know how dangerous the work will be. So too, do Department of Justice officials who warn them to give up any idea of registering voters in Selma, Alabama and get out of town for their own safety.

> I'd actually heard about Selma before [deciding to work there]. It was during the Freedom Rides when the bus I was riding ... was stopped by state police who said it needed to take another route ... because there was a white mob waiting in Selma and they couldn't protect us. I'm saying to myself, 'Oh Lord — even the state troopers are scared of that city.' But even remembering that, I decide I'm going to work in Selma ... and get married. Colia who I married was not afraid of anything. And we married. Our honeymoon was going to be Selma. — Bernard Lafayette. [21]

By February 1963, the Lafayettes are digging in deep, organizing on two fronts. With the help of the Boyntons and other DCVL stalwarts they hold small house meetings of the few adults who have the courage to risk associating with civil rights workers — never more than half a dozen at a time so that the number of parked cars does not attract the notice of Clark's deputies. To avoid snitches, they are careful who they invite, slowly building their network, like hidden tree roots expanding beneath the surface.

They also begin working with local youth, students at the segregated R.B. Hudson High School and Selma University, a small Black Baptist college. As elsewhere in the South, young people without jobs or children to care for are more willing to run risks, and as young freedom fighters themselves, the Lafayettes have enormous prestige. High school student Charles (Chuck) Bonner describes meeting Bernard:

Selma: 1963–1964

One day in February of 1963, when I was 16 years old, my good friend Cleophas Hobbs and I were walking, pushing my mother's green '54 Ford. I had custody of it, it had broken down and we were pushing it ... It was a Sunday. And this young man walked up dressed in a yellow button down shirt, and a tie and a jacket, and he just started to push the car along with us. And simultaneously while we're pushing the car, he said he was Reverend Bernard LaFayette, he was from a seminary up in Tennessee. He had just moved to Selma, and he was from an organization called SNCC. Bernard, was not that much older than we were at the time, he was 22, we were 16.

We then started meeting at the Tabernacle Baptist Church. Bernard suggested that we go back to our high school and tell kids that he was in town. And organize the students. So my dear friend Bettie Mae Fikes was one of the first people we told, and another friend of ours, Evelyn, and another friend Terry Shaw. And they immediately got on board with what Cleo and I were talking about, and went to the Tabernacle Baptist Church and met Bernard. And Bernard taught us various freedom songs ... Bettie then became one of the major leaders in the songs, because she was always the star singer in our high school. — Charles Bonner. [14]

After four months of painstaking, clandestine work, the Lafayettes build enough support to risk coming out of the shadows. In May, Sam Boynton passes on of natural causes, and James Gildersleeve takes over as head of the DCVL. In conjunction with the Lafayettes, the League announces a "Boynton memorial service" at Tabernacle Church. Everyone knows that the service will also be a mass meeting for voter registration and the Freedom Movement. Afraid of white reprisals, the church deacons try to prevent it, but they are forced to relent when Rev. Anderson threatens to hold the service outside and publicly expose their fear.

The Selma Voting Rights Struggle

As evening falls on May 14, Clark, his deputies, and the posse surround Tabernacle Baptist Church to threaten and photograph any who dare attend the meeting. The possemen in their semi-uniform of khaki work clothes, plastic construction helmets, cheap badges, and hate-filled faces, have pistols on their hips and long wooden clubs in their hands. It is an eerie scene as the flashing red and blue lights of the cop cars illuminate the faces of 350 Black citizens who, with sublime courage, overcome their fear, face down the deputies, pass through the posse, and enter the church. But hundreds more who wish to honor Sam Boynton, falter, and turn back rather than run Clark's gauntlet or risk the inevitable Citizens Council retaliation.

Waving a court order from Judge Hare, Clark and some of his deputies invade the church to "prevent insurrection." But neither the audience nor the speakers are intimidated. Jim Forman of SNCC gives the main address, a strong speech, titled "The High Cost of Freedom." Furious at Clark's desecration of their sanctuary and the disrespect he shows to the memory of the much-admired Sam Boynton, the congregation defiantly cheers Forman's in-your-face castigation of Clark and the white power structure. Meanwhile, outside, the deputies and possemen use their clubs to smash the taillights of parked cars. The next day, cops issue tickets to Blacks caught driving with broken lights.

> So Bernard organized his first meeting in honor of Mr. Boynton, who had passed away. And Sheriff Jim Clark surrounded the church, but the most dramatic thing that happened was a group of white men drove up in a truck, and each one was armed with an axe handle. They were actually table legs, they worked at the table factory there in Selma, and they had each come out with these round table legs. That first meeting was very tense, it was at night, we had never had a mass meeting before. We didn't know what a mass meeting was. There was a lot of singing, a lot of praise to Mr. Boynton, a lot of discussion of the need to organize, to challenge the segregation laws, the apartheid laws, but most importantly, the need

Selma: 1963–1964

> to register people to vote. And it was energizing, and it motivated everyone, particularly the students, to get involved in the Movement and to really try to get Black people registered to vote. — Charles Bonner. [14]

More mass meetings follow. Bernard is arrested for "vagrancy." Colia participates in the Birmingham marches and is badly beaten by Bull Connor's cops. Pregnant with their first child, she temporarily returns home to Jackson, Mississippi to recover from internal injuries.

The Selma Times-Journal runs an article on Barnard, identifying who he is, what he is doing, and the exact address where he and Colia live. On the night of June 11, the Klan ambushes Bernard as he returns home from a mass meeting — savagely clubbing him in the head. As he falls to the ground with blood pouring across his face, a Black neighbor comes out with a shotgun, and the Klansmen drive off.

That same night, Medgar Evers is assassinated in Jackson, and federal officials later tell the Lafayettes that the two attacks were part of a coordinated plan to murder Freedom Fighters in three states (the Klan couldn't locate the third target, a CORE worker in Louisiana). Colia is still in Jackson when her friend and mentor Medgar Evers is killed. She helps lead the mass protests that follow.

Bernard is held overnight in the hospital and released the next morning. His face is covered with bruises, eyes swollen half shut, his clothes covered in blood. Rather than retreat home, rather than change into clean clothes, he walks the downtown streets, letting everyone — Black and white — know that he ain't running. His courage gives the lie to charges that SNCC organizers are "outsiders" who will stir up trouble and then flee at the first sign of danger. Courage and hope are the most contagious of all emotions, and from his example, increasing numbers take heart. The mass meetings grow larger, and on registration day twice a month, in twos and threes, Blacks start going down to the courthouse. They are not allowed to become voters, but their defiance begins to break the grip of fear that has imprisoned Selma for generations.

Freedom Day in Selma, 1963

The Lafayettes are joined in Selma by SNCC organizer Prathia Hall — a courageous freedom fighter and fiery orator — who becomes the Black Belt project director when Bernard and Colia return to school in September of '63. Increasing numbers of Dallas County Blacks go to the courthouse to register — they are denied. Thirty-two Black schoolteachers gather their courage and try to register. They are immediately fired. SNCC organizer Worth Long is beaten senseless by a deputy sheriff.

In Birmingham, 120 miles to the north, the 16th Street Baptist Church is bombed on September 15th, killing four little Black girls. The SNCC staff in Selma immediately heads north to stand with the breaved community. Unknown to them, the young people of Selma decide it's time for them to step up. Chuck Bonner recalls:

> The bombing happened and it was all in the news, and Cleo and Terry and I got together, decided we should respond to this, we should take some action in response to this bombing. And we talked to students, we all got together at the Tabernacle Church, and we decided we should have a demonstration. We called the SNCC office ... in Atlanta and we tried to ... get someone to come down, some adult, to help us carry out what was going to be our first demonstration — we had never had a demonstration.
>
> We couldn't get anybody to come down — so we did it anyway. And that's the occasion when Willie C. Robinson went in to Carter's Drug Store along with the other group of demonstrators, and Carter — the owner of the drug store — hit him with an axe handle or some-

Selma: 1963–1964

> thing like that, busted his head, and he had to have seven stitches. Four students were arrested, and then the Movement was on. We immediately organized some other demonstrations, we didn't want those students to be lonely in jail and we sent down another brigade of students, and they were arrested. — Charles Bonner. [14]

Protests continue on the following days; many more students are arrested, over 300 in two weeks. SNCC Chairman John Lewis is thrown in jail for picketing the courthouse in support of voter registration. A teenage girl is knocked off a lunch counter stool and viciously burned with an electric cattle prod as she lays unconscious on the floor.

> SNCC rallied the Black teenagers of Selma and Dallas County and got the students involved. Nonviolent training sessions were held to teach the teens how to act and respond, as well as how not to act and respond when they were attacked or struck by whites. Teenagers who marched were arrested and went to jail with the adults. I was arrested and charged with contributing to the delinquency of minors. ... After arrested teens were released, they would come to the designated church to the evening mass meeting. Parents, upon learning, their child or children had been arrested, would come to the church to get the family member or members. When they came into the church, the parents of the teens who had been arrested would hear old Black men and women testifying about how they were more determined than ever to press forward and secure their rights. Upon hearing these powerful testimonies, the visiting parents would become inspired and join The Movement. — Rev. F.D. Reese, DCVL. [22]

October 7 is the next voter registration day. SNCC and DCVL leaders decide to organize a major mobilization, an all-out effort to get as many potential Black voters as possible down to the

The Selma Voting Rights Struggle

courthouse. They call it a "Freedom Day." Outside supporters are mobilized, SNCC sends in reinforcements, and the national press is alerted.

Comedian and activist Dick Gregory and his wife Lillian come to Selma. She is arrested on a picket line. At mass meeting the night before Freedom Day, armed cops and posse surround the church — as usual. Also as usual, under Judge Hare's court order, Clark and his pistol-toting deputies are in the sanctuary taking note of who is speaking and attending. Gregory electrifies the crowd by denouncing and ridiculing them to their face. High school student Bettie Mae Fikes leads singing that rocks the building, and at midnight author James Baldwin and his brother David arrive to support the Black citizens of Selma.

October 7 — Freedom Day dawns sunny and warm. Historian and activist Howard Zinn records what occurs hour by hour:

> **9:30 am** — Starting at 9 am a line of more than 100 Blacks — some old, some young, most middle-aged — forms outside the Dallas County courthouse door, down the steps, and around the corner. Though menaced by heavily armed Sheriffs deputies and possemen, they do not falter. The line moves with glacial slowness, the registrars are dragging their heels, admitting only a few applicants each hour.
>
> **10 am** — The line is now close to 200. More and more possemen and deputies are arriving, they had not expected such a large turnout. Clark is looking for any excuse to arrest anyone he can on any pretext. Everyone is careful to cross the street at the crosswalk and obey every ordinance.
>
> **10:25 am** — Jim Forman and the Baldwin brothers arrive to support and encourage those on the line. They are ordered to keep moving or be arrested for "blocking the sidewalk."

Selma: 1963–1964

11 am — There are now 290 people on the line. The day is getting hot. No one can leave for water, the "Colored" restrooms are blocked, and it's a violation of segregation laws to use a "white" restroom.

11:40 am — More than 300 are now on the line. After three hours, a total of 12 have been seen by the Registrars and completed the application (it will be days or weeks before they are informed whether they passed — or more likely, "failed" — the Alabama literacy test). Every single person on the line knows that most of them will wait all day until the office closes at 4:30 and never get in the door. They also know that just by being there they are defying a century of white supremecy.

11:50 am — SNCC project director Prathia Hall is arrested at the home of Amelia Boynton on a warrant charging her with "Contributing to the delinquency of minors" — meaning the students arrested for sitting-in at the lunch counters.

11:50am — Three SNCC members stand on the steps of the Federal building across the street from the courthouse. They hold signs saying "Register to Vote." They are immediately arrested and hauled off to jail for "Unlawful assembly." To make the arrests, Clark's deputies have to brush past two Justice Department lawyers and a pair of FBI agents. Howard Zinn asks a Justice Department official: *"Is that a federal building?"* "Yes," the official replies as he turns away. Apparently the Constitutional guarantee of Free Speech applies to neither Alabama nor federal property — at least not so far as the "Department of Justice" is concerned.

12 noon — The Registrars close the office for a two-hour lunch break. There are now 350 Blacks on the line, some have been there since 9 am. The hot sun beats down on them.

The Selma Voting Rights Struggle

12:15 pm — A caravan of gray state trooper cars roar into Selma and fill the street from end to end. Armed with clubs and electric cattle prods, 40 blue-helmeted troopers face off against the determined applicants who are waiting quietly in a single-file line. Again and again, the troopers slap their clubs against their hands, obviously aching to whip heads and make arrests as they did in Birmingham. But the national press is present and Black discipline holds firm, no one responds to the taunts, no one provides a pretext for police mayhem or an excuse that can be used to drive them away from the courthouse. Major Joe Smelley commands the troopers. He issues his orders: anyone who leaves the line for food, water, or a restroom, will not be allowed to rejoin. Nor will anyone be allowed to bring food or water to them. It is a contest of will, a war of endurance.

1:55 pm — Jim Forman and Amelia Boynton tell Sheriff Clark they want to bring food and water to the line. Clark tells them that anyone who tries to do so will be arrested for "molesting" the voter applicants. So too, will anyone who simply tries to talk to them.

2:05 pm — Howard Zinn asks a Justice Department attorney to tell the state troopers that the people waiting on the line are entitled to food and water. *"I won't do it,"* the official replies. *"I believe they do have the right to receive food and water. But I won't do it."* No doubt, he has his orders from Washington.

2:10 pm — Carrying food and water, SNCC field secretaries Avery Williams and Chico Neblett walk toward the line. The troopers attack, knocking them to the ground, beating them with clubs, shocking them with electric cattle prods. As the two SNCC men are taken away, the troopers turn on a newsman, hitting him and knocking down his camera. The line holds. No one leaves.

4:30 pm — The courthouse locks its doors. Hundreds are still waiting on line. [5]

The mass meeting that night is jubilant. Only a few got in to register, and most of them will be denied, but 350 Dallas County Blacks stood toe-to-toe with Clark, the cops, the possemen, and the state troopers. They held their ground. They refused to back down. No one doubts that the struggle ahead will be long and hard, but on this day — this Freedom Day in Selma, Alabama — their quiet, steadfast courage defeated white supremacy. It is a victory and they celebrate it.

Annie Cooper is one of those waiting on the line at the courthouse. She works at a local retirement home. When she comes to work the next day she is fired for trying to register to vote. Some 42 staff members, mostly maids and janitors — Black men and women — walk off the job in protest. They are fired too. All are added to the "blacklist" maintained by the White Citizens Council. No white employer will hire anyone on the list, and there are almost no Black employers. Two weeks later, Annie Cooper is again on the line, trying to register. Month after month, she continues.

The Selma Injunction, 1964

After the high point of Freedom Day in October 1963, Movement activity in Selma begins to ebb. The arrests, trials, and lack of bail money make it difficult for students to continue direct-action protests. As elsewhere in the South, the economic terrorism of the White Citizens Council takes a heavy toll of firings and evictions. Sheriff Clark, his deputies and posse, and their network of snitches instill fear as they continue their efforts to suppress organizing. At the beginning of 1964, Rev. Fredrick D. Reese is elected president of the Dallas County Voter's League

The Selma Voting Rights Struggle

(DCVL). He is a minister and a teacher at the segregated Hudson High School. His courage and determination to resist white supremacy are well known, but against a reign of terror, the going is tough. Spirits sag and attendance at the weekly mass meetings dwindles.

SNCC's small staff tries to carry on, but the organization's resources are stretched thin. Most of its meager funds and the majority of its activists are focused on the struggle in Mississippi — particularly during Freedom Summer. With the support of Father Ouellet SSE (Society of Saint Edmund), volunteers Maria Varela, Silas Norman, James Wiley, Carol Lawson, and Karen House begin an adult literacy project from the St. Elizabeth Parish offices, but its effectiveness is limited by the climate of repression.

In the local community, even the most dedicated Movement supporters are becoming discouraged at the lack of tangible success. All but a few of those who apply to register are denied. The Department of Justice files lawsuit after lawsuit — which they often win in the courts — but those legal victories have no noticeable effect — the white power structure continues to prevent Blacks from voting. When the Lafayettes came to Selma at the end of 1962, roughly 150 of 15,000 eligible Blacks were registered to vote (1%). After enduring two years of struggle, sacrifice, arrests, beatings, firings, and lawsuits, only 335 are registered (2%). As Justice Department official John Doar reports:

> [Even though] the litigation method of correction has been tried harder here than anywhere else in the South, [Dallas County Blacks still have not been provided with] the most fundamental of their constitutional rights — the right to vote." — John Doar.

With enactment of the Civil Rights Act in July 1964, there is a sudden upsurge of hope. On Saturday, July 4, four Black members of SNCC's Selma Literacy Project — Silas Norman, Karen House, Carol Lawson and James Wiley — attempt to implement the new

Selma: 1963–1964

law by desegregating the Thirsty Boy drive-in. A crowd of whites attack them, and they are arrested for "Trespass." At the movie theater, Black students come down from the "Colored" balcony to the white-only main floor. They are also attacked and beaten by whites. The cops close the theater — there will be no integration in Selma, no matter what some federal law in Washington says.

Sunday evening there is a large mass meeting — the first big turnout in months. Sheriff Clark declares the meeting a "riot." Fifty deputies and possemen attack with clubs and tear gas. Monday, July 6, is one of the two monthly voter registration days. SNCC Chairman John Lewis leads a column of voter applicants to the courthouse. They hope the new law will offer them some protection, but Clark herds 50 them into an alley and places them under arrest. As they are marched through the downtown streets to the county jail, the deputies and possemen jab them with clubs and burn them with cattle prods.

On July 9, Judge James Hare issues an injunction forbidding any gathering of three or more people under sponsorship of SNCC, SCLC, or DCVL as organizations, or with the involvement of 41 named leaders including the SNCC organizers, the Boyntons, Marie Foster, Rev. L.L. Anderson, Rev. F.D. Reese, and others. In essence, this injunction makes it illegal to even talk to more than two people at a time about civil rights or voter registration in Selma, Alabama. And because it is an injunction rather than a law, Judge Hare can jail anyone who — in his sole opinion — violates it. And he can do so without the fuss, bother, and expense of a jury trial.

Activists and their attorneys file appeals. They know that on some bright day in the distant future, the blatantly unconstitutional order will eventually be overturned by a higher court. But here and now it paralyzes the Movement. Neither DCVL nor SNCC have the resources — human, financial, legal — to defy the injunction with large-scale civil disobedience. The weekly mass meetings are halted — for the remainder of 1964 there are no public Movement events in Selma, Alabama. The bravest

The Selma Voting Rights Struggle

of the local DCVL leaders continue to meet clandestinely; SNCC organizing is driven deep underground, and a pall of discouragement saps voter registration attempts.

Since mass meetings were now prohibited, we could not rally Black people as in the past. The injunction prohibited mass meetings in churches, but not meetings altogether. Officers of the Dallas County Voter's League and a few local citizens continued meeting after the injunction was issued ... We met in homes and offices to plan. There were eight of us. We became known as the Courageous Eight (Rev. F.D. Reese, Ulysses Blackmon, Amelia Boynton, Ernest Doyle, Marie Foster, James Gildersleeve, Rev. John Hunter, and Rev. Henry Shannon.) — Rev. F.D. Reese, DCVL. [22]

chapter 2

Selma Voting Rights Campaign of 1965

The Situation

As 1964 ends, total Black registration in Dallas County remains at 335, just 2% of the 15,000 who are eligible.

Dallas County, Alabama Voter Registration 1964

Whites Over 21	14,400	49%
Registered White Voters	9,195	64%
Blacks Over 21	15,115	51%
Registered Black Voters	335	2%

Judge Hare's illegal and unconstitutional injunction remains in effect. It prohibits Black leaders and freedom organizations from meeting with three or more people at one time to talk about civil rights or voter registration. Organizing and registration efforts are crippled. There have been no public meetings, no protests,

The Selma Voting Rights Struggle

no mass registration efforts since the injunction was issued six months earlier. Hare's order is being appealed, but the case is moving through the courts with glacial slowness and no victory is in sight.

To discuss voter registration, the small, underfunded SNCC staff in Selma is forced by the injunction to meet with local Blacks in secret. Unable to publicly defy Hare's order, they attempt to circumvent it under cover of freedom schools and adult-literacy efforts, but as a practical matter most voter registration and organizing efforts are stymied. SNCC has been the main national civil rights organization in Selma working with and supporting the local Dallas County Voter's League (DCVL) for the past two years. But most SNCC resources — organizers, money, leadership, focus — are concentrated in Mississippi, first for the Freedom Summer Project and then for the follow-up MFDP Congressional Challenge.

As in Alabama, Blacks in Mississippi are denied voting rights and barred from participating in the Democratic Party. In order to press its demand for civil rights and full citizenship, the Freedom Movement in that state organize the Mississippi Freedom Democratic Party (MFDP) as an alternate political organization which people can join regardless of whether or not they are legally registered to vote. Though it's primarily a Black group, people of all races are welcome in the MFDP.

The white-only Democrats in Mississippi operate in flagrant violation of national Democratic Party rules. Working in strict accordance to those rules, the MFDP elects delegates to the 1964 national Democratic convention in Atlantic City, NJ. They ask that the national party recognize them as representatives from their state. Even though the all-white Mississippi delegates support Barry Goldwater the Republican candidate, President Lyndon B. Johnson denies the MFDP claim for fear of offending white voters in the South by seating a Black-led delegation in the place of the white-only "Dixiecrats." After the November election, the MFDP brings a challenge in Congress to the seating of white Representatives elected from Mississippi. Charging that their election was fraudulent because Blacks were denied the right to vote and participate in party politics, they commence a process under House rules to force a new election. Ultimately, the challenge fails, but the testimony and investigation it engenders help push forward eventual passage of the Voting Rights Act.

The Alabama Project

Back in September of '63, when four young girls were killed in the Birmingham bombing of the 16th Street Baptist church, Diane Nash Bevel drew up a "Proposal for Action in Montgomery" — a plan for a massive direct action assault on segregation and denial of voting rights. The plan called for building and training a nonviolent army 20-40,000 strong who would engage in large-scale civil disobedience by blocking roads, airports, and government buildings to demand the removal of Governor George Wallace and the immediate registration of every Alabama citizen over the age of 21. When she presents the idea to Dr. Martin Luther King, she tells him, *"..you can tell people not to fight only if you offer them a way by which justice can be served without violence."* Rev. C.T. Vivian and SNCC & CORE activists support the idea, but King and most of his other advisors do not consider it feasible.

A month later, Diane and James Bevel again raise the plan, later called the "Alabama Project," at a board meeting of the Southern Christian Leadership Conference (SCLC). The general concept of some kind of "March on Montgomery" some time in the future is supported, but no date is set, no specific plans made, and there is no consensus around the idea of militant direct action and massive civil disobedience. Instead, SCLC's attention focuses on continuing the struggle in Birmingham and the situation in Danville VA.

In November of '63, the assassination of President John F. Kennedy and the intensifying FBI COINTELPRO attack on the Freedom Movement and Dr. King disrupt all plans.

The Selma Voting Rights Struggle

The FBI's Counter Intelligence Program — generally known as COINTELPRO — was an illegal, covert effort to undermine and destroy individuals and organizations whose politics offended Bureau Director J. Edgar Hoover. Between 1956 and 1971, FBI agents were ordered to, "expose, disrupt, misdirect, discredit, or otherwise neutralize," the activities of American political groups and individuals who were engaged in legal, Constitutionally-protects efforts to end racism, reform economic abuses, and extend democracy. Liberals and progressives were discredited and smeared with forged documents and false reports leaked to news media, employers were pressured fire them, some were framed and sent to prison on false charges. Organizations such as SCLC, SNCC, and CORE were spied on, wire-tapped, infiltrated, disrupted, and sabotaged. Many civil rights activists believed that in carrying out COINTELPRO directives some FBI agents worked with White Citizens Councils engaged in economic retaliation against Blacks who attempted to register to vote, and may have encouraged and abetted the Klan in violent attacks against civil rights activists.

In February of 1964, the Bevels again put their proposal for a prolonged nonviolent campaign to win enfranchisement before Dr. King, adding to it the idea of petitioning Congress to reduce the number of Alabama House members until Black citizens are allowed to vote. An SCLC meeting in March supports the idea, though with Birmingham as the target city rather than Montgomery because of noncompliance by the white power structure with the agreement that had ended the 1963 Birmingham protests. But no specific plans are made.

By the Spring of 1964, the so-called "white backlash" against rising Black assertiveness is swelling, and Goldwater's presidential campaign endorsing "states rights" is gaining ground. So too is George Wallace's campaign challenging LBJ in the Democratic primaries.

In the context of the 1960s, "states rights" means the right of individual states to impose mandatory racial segregation laws, restrict voting rights, and ignore (or "nullify") race-related

1965 Campaign

Supreme Court rulings that state leaders disliked.

Fearful of upsetting white voters who might support Goldwater, some northern liberals and conservative Black leaders call for a "moratorium" on all forms of direct action until after the November elections. When Brooklyn CORE calls for a freeway "stall-in" on the opening day of the New York World's Fair, many condemn the action. Dr. King refuses to join the critics:

Frankly, I have gotten a little fed-up with the lectures that we are now receiving from the white power structure, even when it comes from such true and tried friends as [Senators] Humphrey, Kuchel, Javits and Keating. ... [Somehow demonstrations] always become wrong and 'ill-timed' when they are engaged in by the Negro. ... Indeed, we are engaged in a social revolution, and while it may be different from other revolutions, it is a revolution just the same. It is a movement to bring about certain basic structural changes in the architecture of American society. This is certainly revolutionary. My only hope is that it will remain a nonviolent revolution. ... We do not need allies who are more devoted to order than to justice. ... Neither do we need allies who will paternalistically seek to set the time-table for our freedom. ... If our direct action programs alienate so-called friends ... they never were real friends. — Martin Luther King.[6]

In the U.S. Senate, opposition to the pending Civil Rights bill is fierce.

Instead of initiating a new voting rights campaign in Alabama, SCLC decides in late Spring to maintain pressure on Congress by throwing most of its strength into reinforcing the on-going anti-segregation campaign in St. Augustine, FL. The Bevels, James Orange, and a few other members of SCLC's small field staff, begin organizing in Birmingham, Montgomery, and Tuscaloosa where a new direct action struggle erupts. But as a practical matter the "Alabama Project" is put on the shelf.

In November 1964, with the Civil Rights Act passed and Goldwater defeated, the Bevels again raise the "Alabama Project," arguing that the time has come to move on voting rights —

The Selma Voting Rights Struggle

which cannot be won without national legislation that eliminates "literacy tests" and strips power from county registrars. Such legislation, they argue, can only be won through mass action in the streets.

Meanwhile, in Selma, the injunction continues to stymie Movement activity. Long-time freedom fighter Amelia Boynton tells SCLC that if they are serious about voting rights in Alabama, they should come to Selma and defy the injunction. Rev. C.T. Vivian is sent to consult with DCVL and other Black leaders in Selma.

> In late 1964, SNCC's finances were dwindling. This organization was also beginning to experience internal differences regarding philosophies. The organization's effectiveness was waning in Dallas County. ... Those of us who had the vision knew the Movement in Dallas County had to be elevated to another level. We had no choice. Representatives of the Dallas County Voter's League and several local citizens met at the home of Mrs. Amelia Boynton one evening. Mrs. Boynton was an extremely courageous woman. Her husband was the president of the Dallas County Voter's League before I was elected. The Courageous Eight invited representatives from the Southern Christian Leadership Conference (SCLC) to the meeting at Mrs. Boynton's home. It was at this meeting that we formally invited SCLC and Dr. Martin Luther King, Jr. to come to Selma. — Rev. F.D. Reese, DCVL. [22]

The decision is made. DCVL becomes the SCLC affiliate in Selma and SCLC commits to a voting rights campaign in Alabama with an initial focus on Selma and then expanding into rural Black Belt counties.

> We wanted to raise the issue of voting to the point where we could take it outside of the Black Belt ... We were us-

ing Selma as a way to shake Alabama ... so that it would no longer be a Selma issue or even an Alabama issue but a national issue. — C.T. Vivian. [6]

Saturday, January 2, 1965, is set as the date for defying the injunction and commencing a massive direct action campaign. There are no illusions. Selma, Dallas County, and the Alabama Black Belt are bastions of white supremacy and violent resistance to Black aspirations. Everyone understands that when you demand the right to vote in Alabama you put your life — and the lives of those who join you — on the line.

SCLC and SNCC

Both nationally and in Selma, relations between SNCC and SCLC are tense. SNCC staff have been working and organizing in Selma for two years, enduring hardship, danger, brutality, and jail to slowly build an organizational foundation. They deeply resent SCLC coming in to use that foundation for a kind of large-scale mobilization that they distrust. SCLC counters that Selma's local leaders have asked for their help because the injunction has halted progress for six months.

Once close allies in the southern struggle, the two organizations are now on divergent paths. Dr. King and SCLC are still deeply committed to nonviolence, integration, multiracial activism, and appeals to the conscience of the nation. But after years of liberal indifference, federal inaction, and political betrayal, many in SNCC now question, and in some cases explicitly reject, some or all of those concepts.

SNCC is oriented toward building grassroots community organizations led by those at the bottom of society. Rather than seeing themselves as leaders, SNCC field secretaries view themselves as community organizers empowering local people to take control over their own lives. For its part, SCLC maintains that the community is already organized around the Black church, that ministers are, and always have been, the accepted community heads, and that the focus should be on moving those churches and preachers into social- political action. SNCC argues back that the ministers and congregation leaders are primarily concerned with issues affecting the Black elite and they do little for the sharecroppers, maids, and laborers who fill the pews. SCLC responds that splitting Black communities into rival camps weakens everyone and aids no one.

SNCC field secretaries toil anonymously in the most dangerous areas of the South with little or no media coverage or recognition, and they deeply resent the flood of publicity and adulation bestowed on Dr. King when he visits locales where they have been working for years. Some SNCC members express that bitterness by referring to him in a mocking tone as *"De Lawd."*

Though King accepts such derision with easy grace, other SCLC leaders and staff bristle with hostility. In SNCC's view, local Black communities can provide their own leaders and that media-centric, "big-name" outsiders like King not only hinder that process but are unnecessary. To SCLC, nationally-recognized spokesmen who can articulate the Freedom Movement to the world are essential, and some openly scoff at what they see as SNCC's over-idealization of local activism, noting that whenever King speaks in a Black community it is those very same local people who flood the aisles to overflowing.

In SCLC's view, the only way to substantially change the lives of those at the bottom of society is to win transformative national legislation like the Civil Rights Act. SNCC sees little value in federal laws that are weakly enforced and that, in any case, do not even attempt to address the grinding poverty of the great majority of the Black population. Without strong organizations of their own, poor Blacks will remain powerless regardless of laws passed in Washington. To counter this, SNCC's strategy is deep community organizing to build local political power at the grassroots.

1965 Campaign

SCLC's position is that without the vote no community organization can wield effective power; therefore poverty cannot be addressed until Blacks at all economic levels have the ballot. In their view, voting rights can only be achieved through decisive national legislation, and that only large-scale, direct action mobilizations like Birmingham and St. Augustine can overcome white resistance to Black voting rights and force Congress to act. SNCC opposes such mobilization campaigns, saying they inevitably result in mass arrests and increased white terror, both of which disrupt and divert the slow, delicate organizing process. They accuse SCLC of bringing in their own leaders who then fail to leave viable local organizations behind when they move on to the next campaign. SCLC activists deny SNCC's contention, arguing that Black churches and community coalitions like the Alabama Christian Movement for Human Rights are the continuing foundation of community activism.

In order to win legislation at the national level, SCLC has to influence and maintain ties with the Johnson administration and the northern-liberal wing of the Democratic Party. But LBJ and those same liberals betrayed the MFDP at the 1964 Democratic Convention in Atlantic City and SNCC wants nothing more to do with them. Instead, they have turned toward building independent Black-led political organizations outside the Democratic Party, which puts them in direct conflict with some national party leaders who still hope to retain southern Electoral College votes that are essential to keeping a Democrat in the White House.

On a practical organizational level, unlike the NAACP and CORE who have dues-paying members in self-sustaining chapters, both SCLC and SNCC rely on fund appeals and donations from supporters — often the same groups and individuals — which puts them in direct competition for with each other for desperately needed financial resources.

These differences are deeply felt and passionately argued. As 1965 dawns, they remain unresolved.

The Selma Voting Rights Struggle

Selma on the Eve

In the middle of December 1964, SCLC project director James Bevel meets in Montgomery with John Love, SNCC's Selma project director, along with Dave Dennis and Ike Reynolds of CORE to gain their support for the voting rights campaign. The meeting does not go well. Bevel is arrogant and dismissive of views other than his own. There is no agreement.

On December 28, Dr. King convenes a much larger meeting where he presents the SCLC plan, now called the "Project for an Alabama Political Freedom Movement." The proposal is to break the Selma injunction on January 2, engage in mass action and voter registration in Dallas County, and then spread out into the rural counties of the Alabama Black Belt. By spring, the campaign is to evolve into a freedom registration and freedom ballot campaign similar to what SNCC and its allies organized in Mississippi, culminating on May 4 in a direct action and legal challenge to the seating of the entire Alabama state legislature on grounds similar to those of the MFDP Congressional Challenge.

Bob Moses and Ivanhoe Donaldson of SNCC argue against the SCLC proposal. Instead, they urge support for the MFDP's congressional challenge. But local leaders and activists from Selma and elsewhere in Alabama strongly endorse SCLC's plan and commit themselves to it. The ministers of Brown Chapel, Tabernacle, and First Baptist courageously pledge their churches for meeting space in defiance of the injunction.

As 1964 draws to a close, SCLC's small field staff — Jim Bevel and Diane Nash Bevel, James Orange, Andrew Marrisett, Willie Bolden, Lester Hankerson, and a handful of others — set up in Selma and begin mobilizing for the January 2nd mass meeting. Already in Selma are a band of SNCC organizers, some of whom have been there for months and years. Among them: John Love, Worth Long, Avery Williams, Prathia Hall, Silas Norman, and Maria Varela.

Years of struggle and danger have forged a cadre of determined

1965 Campaign

local leaders: Amelia Boynton; the reverends F.D. Reese and L.L. Anderson; school teacher Margaret Moore; attorney J.L. Chestnut; dentist Dr. Sullivan Jackson, and his sister Marie Foster, the local head of SCLC's Citizenship Schools, and many others, such as Claude Brown, Ernest Doyle, James Gildersleeve, J.D. Hunter, and Ulysses Blackman.

The one thing SNCC did not have to do in Selma was identify and develop grassroots community leadership. As I said, this was a self-contained community, and its Dallas County Voter's League had a mighty impressive group of leaders. Some proud, fearless black leaders who, against all odds, had never quit and never backed down. Nuff respect. They were mostly professional people: ministers like the Reverend Mr. Lewis and the Reverend Mr, Reese; Dr. Jackson, who I believe was a dentist; tough-talking, indefatigable attorney J. L. Chestnutt; and of course, the president, Mrs. Amelia Boynton, a former teacher and widely respected leader.

> A word about that family. Mrs. Boynton was a gracious, elegantly spoken lady. A teacher deeply committed to her people's uplift; Mrs. Boynton had been president of the Dallas County NAACP. When the NAACP was outlawed in Alabama, she didn't miss a beat. She merely led the membership into the Voters League and became president of that. She was demure, highly "cultured," and quite unintimidatable. The entire Boynton family were warriors. The plaintiff in the Supreme Court case Boynton vs. Virginia, which integrated interstate bus travel, was her son. Her husband also had been a highly respected leader, who managed — with the ingenuity of his widow — to continue the fight literally from his grave. — Kwame Ture (Stokely Carmichael). [1]

And eagerly awaiting action are Selma's young warriors — high school and college students who have already born the brunt of confrontation and jail: Charles (Chuck) Bonner, Bettie Mae Fikes, Cleophus Hobbs, Terry Shaw, Evelyn Mann, Thomasina

The Selma Voting Rights Struggle

Marshall, Willie Emma Scott, and many others.

An old, three-story brick building occupies the corner of Alabama Avenue and Franklin Street. On the ground floor is a Black funeral parlor, above it are the main offices of Selma's freedom organizations. Directly across the street is Selma city hall with both the city and county jails on the upper floors. If the blinds are open, it's possible to look from the windows of one building into the other.

Inside city hall and over at the county courthouse, the white power structure cannot agree on how to handle the direct action campaign that SCLC has just publicly announced. Newly elected Mayor Smitherman, a local refrigerator salesman, is a "moderate" segregationist. He hopes to attract northern business investment — Hammermill Paper of Pennsylvania is considering Selma as the location for a big new plant, but they will shy away if "racial troubles" shine a spotlight of negative media on the town. Smitherman has appointed veteran lawman Wilson Baker to head the city's 30-man police force. They and their supporters believe that the most effective method of countering civil rights protests (and avoiding bad press) is to *"kill 'em with kindness"* as Police Chief Laurie Pritchett did in Albany, Georgia a few years earlier.

Short-tempered Sheriff Jim Clark and arch-segregationist Judge Hare furiously disagree. They and their hard-line, white supremacy faction are committed to maintaining southern apartheid through brutal repression. As they see it, billy clubs, electric cattle-prods, whips, jail cells, and charging horses, are what is needed to keep the Coloreds in line — and if Yankee business interests don't like it, they can take their investments elsewhere.

These two factions are at war with each other. Baker narrowly lost to Clark in the sheriff's race, carrying the (white) city vote but not the rural areas. Now they angrily spar over jurisdiction. Baker's cops patrol the city except for the block where the county courthouse sits, which Clark and his deputies control. Outside the city limits, Clark and his volunteer posse reign supreme.

1965 Campaign

Breaking the Selma Injunction

On New Year's Day, January 1, 1965, Bevel meets with Black leaders in Selma to prepare for breaking the injunction on the morrow. The January 2nd date is chosen because Sheriff Clark will be out of town at the Orange Bowl football game in Miami. Chief Baker has stated that city police under his command will not enforce Judge Hare's illegal injunction, and without Clark to lead them, there is little chance that sheriff's deputies will break up the mass meeting on their own.

The day before the scheduled Mass Meeting it snowed. On 2 January 1965, the first Mass Meeting since July 1964 was held at Brown Chapel. When the injunction was imposed in the summer of 1964, mass meetings were suspended by the courts and there were no such gatherings in Selma for six months.

When we decided to resume the mass meetings in January 1965, all of the local pastors declined to host the initial meeting at their church. Brown Chapel was the only church that opened its doors to the people. This is how Brown Chapel African Methodist Episcopal Church in Selma became famous and her long time reputation for the cause of Christ remained unblemished. ...

> Around 3:00 p.m. on 2 January 1965 we thought no one was going to show for the mass meeting. ... Slowly the people started coming into the church. The Courageous Eight had given every indication that we were ready to go to jail. Law enforcement officers were present to see how many people would turn out. More people turned out than the city authorities expected. They did not arrest us. There were too many Black people inside and outside of Brown Chapel to be confined to the Selma City Jail. — Rev. F.D. Reese, DCVL. [22]

The mass meeting is a huge success. Some 700 Black citizens from Selma, Dallas County, and the surrounding Black Belt fill Brown Chapel to overflowing. They are determined to defy the injunction, determined to be free. Also in the audience are

The Selma Voting Rights Struggle

numerous reporters and both state and local cops. Clark is not yet back from Miami and no effort is made to enforce the injunction. Dr. King tells them:

> Today marks the beginning of a determined, organized, mobilized campaign to get the right to vote everywhere in Alabama. If we are refused we will appeal to Governor George Wallace. If he refuses to listen, we will appeal to the legislature. If they don't listen, we will appeal to the conscience of Congress. ... We must be ready to march. We must be ready to go to jail by the thousands. ... Our cry to the state of Alabama is a simple one. Give us the ballot! — Martin Luther King, Jr. [7]

After the rally, King, local Black leaders, SCLC and SNCC staff meet at Mrs. Boynton's home to plan the next steps. Now that the injunction has been defied without arrests or violence, the focus turns to the demand for voting rights. The voter registration office at the courthouse is only open on alternate Mondays — the next date is January 18. That gives two weeks to recruit, organize, and train voter applicants to show up *en masse* to register.

On Sunday the 3rd, King leaves for speaking engagements, fundraising events, and meetings to organize national support. Diane Nash Bevel coordinates SCLC and SNCC staff, now operating in pairs, who fan out through Selma's Black neighborhoods, canvassing door-to-door to talk about voter registration. Though fear is still pervasive, a few courageous souls step forward. On Thursday, January 7, evening meetings and workshops with prospective registrants are held in each of Selma's five electoral wards. Sheriff's deputies barge into some of the meetings to "observe." Bevel electrifies the 50 participants at the Ward IV meeting in Brown Chapel by ordering them out of the building. They leave. The next day, some 200 students attend a youth rally. On Tuesday the 12th, ward meetings of up to 100 begin electing block captains.

Bernard Lafayette, SNCC's first Selma organizer who has close ties to both SNCC and SCLC, arrives from Chicago to help ease friction between the two organizations. Hosea Williams of SCLC and John Lewis of SNCC are now in Selma. SNCC and SCLC field staff reinforcements begin to arrive — Fay Bellamy, Frank Soracco, Charles Fager, and others. Silas Norman is appointed SNCC's new Selma project director and former Selma student, now SNCC staff member, Terry Shaw becomes coordinator for Ward III.

King returns to Selma on Thursday, January 14, to address a large mass meeting at First Baptist. He declares Monday a "Freedom Day" when direct action is to commence with a mass march to the courthouse by voter applicants. *"If we march by the hundreds, we will make it clear to the nation that we are determined to vote."* Volunteers will also apply for "white-only" city jobs, and integration teams will attempt to implement the Civil Rights Act by demanding service at segregated facilities — the first such action since students were beaten and arrested the previous July.

On Friday, January 15 — Dr. King's 36th birthday — a band of Black teenagers skip the Hudson High basketball game to tell movement leaders they intend to ditch school and march on Monday. Big James Orange of SCLC, former high-school football star and Birmingham student leader, tells them to be at Brown Chapel on Monday.

Marching to the Courthouse

Under Alabama law at this time, voter registration is a complex process. First, you have to fill out a four-page Alabama Voter Application. Then you take a so-called "Alabama Literacy Test." Then you have to find someone who is already a registered voter to "vouch" for you, and after all that, you still have to wait days or weeks to find out if the Registrars — in their sole subjective opinion — judge you fit to be a voter. These requirements are rigorously enforced against Blacks, but usually ignored for whites who are permitted to register without hindrance.

The Selma Voting Rights Struggle

SELMA: On Monday morning, January 18, Black citizens gather at Brown Chapel. After freedom songs, prayers, and speeches, Dr. King and John Lewis lead 300 marchers out of the church in Selma's first protest action since the injunction. Some are courageous adults determined to become voters, others are students for whom freedom is more important than attending class. They walk two-by-two on the Sylvan Street sidewalk (today, Sylvan Street is Martin Luther King Street). Police Chief Wilson Baker quickly halts the line. They have no permit for a "parade," but he agrees to allow them to walk in small groups to the courthouse. In other words, he is not enforcing Judge Hare's "three-person" injunction, but neither is he allowing Blacks to exercise their Constitutional right to peacefully march in protest.

Judge Hare and Sheriff Clark are furious at Baker's "betrayal." Clark, his deputies, and his posse, wait at the courthouse where they — not Baker — have jurisdiction. They bar the main courthouse entrance on Alabama Avenue and herd the Blacks into a back alley out of sight (local whites, of course, are freely allowed in through the front door). In the alley, Blacks wait all day for a chance to fill out the voter application and take the literacy test. As they stand in the cold, they know they are risking far more than just humiliation and abuse. Many of those who tried to register during Freedom Day in October 1963 were evicted from their homes or fired from their jobs. Amelia Boynton, a registered voter, stands by to vouch for anyone who manages to get that far in the process, but since the Registrar is "too busy" for any Blacks to apply, Mrs. Boynton waits in vain.

Meanwhile, integration teams test facilities in downtown. Everyone is served in compliance with the Civil Rights Act. King, Rev. Fred L. Shuttlesworth, and other Black leaders check in for a night at the ornate, historically "white-only," Hotel Albert. While talking in the lobby with Dorothy Cotton, Dr. King is knocked to the floor and kicked by a leader of the National States Rights Party who is quickly arrested by Wilson Baker.

The next day, Tuesday, January 19, Black voter applicants and

1965 Campaign

student supporters return to the courthouse even though the registration office is closed and won't open again for two weeks. This time they are not taken by surprise, and many refuse orders to wait in the back alley — they insist on using the front door on Alabama Avenue. First in line and first to be arrested are Hosea Williams of SCLC and John Lewis of SNCC. Amelia Boynton is again present to vouch. Sheriff Clark grabs her by the neck and manhandles her into a police car. Clark's deputies surround those trying to use the main entrance. They use their electric cattle-prods to herd everyone down Alabama Avenue toward the county jail. Among them is 3rd-grader Sheyann Webb (age 8), who recalls:

> I was the youngest, certainly the smallest, of the "regulars" in the demonstrations. ... I was with Mrs. Margaret Moore again.. ... Deputies with sticks and those long cattle prods moved toward us. I squeezed tight on Mrs. Moore's hand; there was a sudden urge to back away, even turn and run. Somebody shouted, "Y'all are under arrest!" I looked up at Mrs. Moore, *"Me, too? Are they arrestin' me?" "Don't be scared,"* she said. *"Don't let go of my hand."* I saw some of them deputies push our people, saw some of them use the cattle prods and saw men and women jump when the electric ends touched against their bodies. ... My toes were stepped on and I lost my balance several times as we were wedged together. Then they ... began marching us down Alabama Avenue, back toward the [county jail]. I was now holding onto Mrs. Moore with both of my hands, watching so I wouldn't get touched with one of the prods. We were being moved like cattle. ... [At the jail] an officer came up to me and asked why I was there. *"To be free,"* I said.
> — Sheyann Webb. [9]

Sheyann is released and allowed to return home, but more than 60 others are charged. Lawyers from the NAACP Legal Defense Fund manage to get them released pending trial in time to attend

43

The Selma Voting Rights Struggle

the evening mass meeting where they are honored as heroes.

The following day, Wednesday, January 20, applicants and supporters march to the courthouse in three sequential waves, each one carefully broken into small groups to conform to Baker's decree forbidding "parades." They insist on using the Alabama Street entrance and are all arrested by Jim Clark. Among them is Rev. L.L. Anderson of Tabernacle Baptist, the first minister to open his church for civil rights activity back in 1963. By the end of this third day, some 225 have been incarcerated. A sheriff's deputy cracks wise, *"Jim Clark 225, Martin Luther Coon, zero!"*

> The office hours for the courthouse were 9 am to 12 noon. The White workers went to lunch and official business was resumed from 2 pm to 4 pm. Some days only 25 or 30 Black people were interviewed and none in that number were registered. The Black citizens kept coming day after day in spite of the schemes that had been designed to frustrate them. ... After standing in line to be interviewed and being beaten cruelly by the sheriff and his deputies and then being arrested; the people would testify at the evening mass meeting: "I came scared, but I feel good bout what I did t' day and I'm ready t' go to jail again." — Rev. F.D. Reese, DCVL. [22]

WASHINGTON: On this day when Black citizens in Selma — many of them combat veterans of World War II and Korea — are being denied not only the right to vote but their Constitutional right to freedom of speech and peaceful assembly, President Johnson is inaugurated in Washington before a huge throng of supporters. Leontyne Price is invited to sing *America the Beautiful,* and a White House spokesman brags that this is *"The first Inauguration where every operation [is] integrated from the church to the ballroom."*

But Johnson's speech contains only a single, vaguely worded, platitude alluding to racial justice. Though many Black leaders and some civil rights activists attend inaugural balls and events, Dr. King is not among them. He has declined all inaugural invitations and remains in Selma.

The Teachers March

SELMA: Throughout the South, inadequate segregated school systems and grinding poverty prevent all but a small handful of Blacks from ever attending college. Those who do achieve a college degree and remain in the region are the educated elite, the intellectual leaders of their communities. But few middle-class positions in the South are open to Black graduates, so most become teachers in "Colored" schools. Though Black teachers are paid less than whites, their incomes are still significantly higher than the sharecroppers, maids, and laborers who comprise the overwhelming majority of the Black community.

In the South, teachers have no unions to protect them. Black teachers can be fired at will by white school boards, and the White Citizens Council stands ever vigilant to root out "agitators" and "trouble-makers." In many southern states, membership in the NAACP is legal grounds for immediate, mandatory dismissal, as is any other form of civil rights activity — or even just trying to register to vote. As a result, while many Black teachers clandestinely support the Freedom Movement, few are willing to sacrifice their financial security by risking any sort of public participation.

But in Selma, a few school teachers such as Rev. F.D. Reese and Margaret Moore defy the school board and Citizens Council by assuming leadership roles. As the 1965 voting rights campaign intensifies with nightly mass meetings, marches to the courthouse, and students walking out of school to face arrest, Reese, Moore and a few others begin organizing and mobilizing the Black teachers. They challenge their colleagues, *"How can we teach American civics if we ourselves cannot vote?"* One by one, teachers sign a pledge that they will go together to the courthouse and attempt to register as a group.

The Selma Voting Rights Struggle

Friday, January 22, is the day. After school, they gather at Clark Elementary School in their Sunday best — the women in hats, gloves, and high-heels, the men in somber suits. Reese takes roll of those who have promised to march. They are all present. They know they not only risk losing their jobs, they risk arrest — hundreds have already been jailed for trying to register to vote.

> The sheriff will think twice about mistreating you. You are teachers in the public school system of the state of Alabama, but you can't vote. We're going to see about that today. If they put us in jail, there won't be anybody to teach the children. [Clark] knows if they're not in school, then they'll be out in the streets. — Rev. F.D. Reese. [9]

Some of the teachers hold up a toothbrush, a visible symbol of their willingness to face jail. Solemnly, silently, 110 of them — almost every Black teacher in Selma — march to the courthouse in small groups as required by Baker. Nowhere in the South, not ever, not in Nashville, not in Albany or Birmingham, not in Durham, Jackson, or St. Augustine have teachers publicly marched as teachers.

Clark Elementary was located in front of the G.W. Carver Homes which were the projects where poverty stricken Black families resided. Parents came out of their simple dwellings to encourage us. Old ladies and old men walked slowly from inside their homes, and stood in front yards and near the sidewalk. The faces of men and women who had, due to their will power and faith, survived under one of the most oppressive and discriminatory systems in a Southern town met our eyes. It is difficult to say to whom this march meant the most, the teachers or the observers.

> The students who were home from school by this time cheered with delight as the rhythm of our footsteps signaled our intention to execute the plan. Black mothers held their babies and watched with great satisfaction

1965 Campaign

> as we marched toward the courthouse. Many Black bystanders in the projects were weeping and sobbing openly as we passed by their homes. They were outwardly shaken by the sound of our footsteps, knowing the teachers were not going to turn around. Many of the weeping bystanders had been arrested on numerous occasions during the past 12 to 18 months, while the teachers had only been exposed to minimal discomforts and abuses. — Rev. F.D. Reese, DCVL. [22]

At the courthouse, Clark and his deputies wait. They wear pistols on sagging belts and carry cattle prods and hardwood billy clubs which they smack against their palms in anticipation. At 3:30 in the afternoon the first group approaches. Led by Reese, they walk two-by-two up the steps of the Alabama Avenue entrance. They will not go into the back alley; they will enter by the front or not at all. As each group arrives, the line snaking down the street grows longer. School Superintendent J.A. Pickard, and Edgar Stewart the School Board president (and a former FBI agent) confront them — the Registrar's is office closed, their request to register after class is denied. Go home.

> We refused to move. After one minute or so the sheriff took it upon himself to move us. He drew back and began jabbing me and Durgan in the stomach. The deputies immediately imitated the sheriff's behavior. They began jabbing other teachers and wildly pushing us down the concrete steps. We began to fall back like bowling pins. The teachers grunted, bent over involuntarily as the blows from the clubs registered, and breathed heavily while falling. The strikes from the billy clubs stung. No mercy was shown to the women. The teachers had no weapons and desired none. Determination and will power were our weapons of choice. Clark and his men successfully cleared the front of the courthouse of marchers from the top step to the bottom. — Rev. F.D. Reese, DCVL. [22]

The Selma Voting Rights Struggle

With help from SCLC field secretary "Big Lester" Hankerson, Reese reforms the line and leads them back up the steps to the doors. Again, the cops drive them down. Again, they reform and rise up to the doors that are barred against them.

Clark threatens to arrest them all, but wiser heads prevail. The Circuit Solicitor pulls him inside and can be seen through the glass speaking urgently to him. Until now, only a few hundred Black students have participated in the protests, but if the Black teachers are all in jail, come Monday there could be thousands in the streets. Clark orders the teachers shoved back down the steps a third time. This time, Reese and SCLC leader Andrew Young decide the point has been made. Instead of trying again, the teachers march in their small groups back to Brown Chapel where a throng of their students wait to greet them.

> Most of us had viewed the educators as stodgy old people, classic examples of true "Uncle Toms." But that wasn't the opinion that day. I looked about me and saw scores of other children running about the [Carver Housing Project] shouting the news that Mr. Somebody or Old Mrs. Somebody was marching. Could you believe it?
>
> Some little boys came running down the street yelling that they were coming back. Me and Rachel [West] went into the church which was packed with people. We waited and when the teachers began coming in everybody in there just stood up and applauded. Then somebody started to sing ... first one song and then another, as they walked in. And they were all smiling; kids were shaking hands with their teachers and hugging them. I had never seen anything like that before ...
>
> Some of the women teachers were crying, they were so elated. Mrs. Bright spotted me, and rushed forward, hugging me. She appeared to be in a mood of triumph.

> She laughed, she wiped at her eyes, she hugged me again. I remember she said something about her feet being tired, and I said, "You did real good. — Sheyann Webb. [9]

Annie Cooper and Sheriff Clark

SELMA: Over the weekend, U.S District Judge Daniel Thomas in Mobile — a native Alabamian with scant sympathy for Black civil rights — issues rules that permit Clark to continue forcing Black voter applicants to line up in the alley, but he requires that at least 100 must be permitted to wait without being arrested. On Monday, January 25, Dr. King leads marchers to the courthouse where they line up two-by-two as ordered by Thomas. Soon the line grows to 250 or more. Clark orders that all marchers in excess of 100 be dispersed. SNCC worker Willie McRae disputes this interpretation of the judge's ruling and is immediately arrested. He goes limp, and is dragged off to a police car.

Some of the Black voter applicants turn to see what is going on. Sheriff Clark strides down the sidewalk forcing them back into line. One of them is Annie Lee Cooper (54) who, along with a co-worker, was fired from her job at Dunn's Rest Home after they tried to register back in October of 1963. When their boss not only terminated them but subjected them to insult and physical abuse, 38 of their fellow workers — Black women all — walked off the job in protest. They too were fired and their photos circulated among potential white employers. Now, 15 months later, most remain unemployed. Clark twists Cooper's arm and shoves her hard; she hauls off and slugs him with her fist. He is driven to his knees and she hits him again. Mrs. Cooper recalled:

> I saw Jim Clark fling Mrs. Boynton around like a leaf a day or two before. Clark was larger than I on the outside, but I was larger than he on the inside. The altercation started. ... Jim Clark could not take me down alone.

The Selma Voting Rights Struggle

The town sheriff and I were going at it blow for blow, punch for punch, and lick for lick, with our fists. It was a plain old street brawl. Suddenly he cried out to his deputies: "Don'y' an see this nigger woman beatin' me? Do some'um." At the urging of the sheriff the others came to his aid. All four of them closed in on me.

Clark took his nightstick and prepared to land a blow. Before he knew it, I had his arm and held it back with a tight grip. Clark brought his billy club over my face. He managed to put enough power in his swing to graze me across the upper part of my eye with the nightstick. The blow stung and was hard enough to draw blood. It struck me over my eye. I was fiercely holding his hand so he could not strike me again. I heard Dr. King urging the marchers to stay calm. He was afraid the marchers were going to turn violent while watching the Policemen attack me. It was four against one. It took everything each of the four had to manhandle me.

The deputies wrestled me down onto the pavement, as the crowd looked on. Clark planted his knee in my stomach, as the deputies had me on my back. That was the only way he could have gotten his knee in my stomach. He stood no chance of wrestling me to the ground alone. The deputies rolled me over on my stomach and handcuffed my hands behind my back. They lifted me to my feet and took me to the paddy-wagon. I was taken through an alley in town. While walking through the alley, Clark took his billy club and landed a blow on my head. It was a fierce lick. The blow cracked my skull. ...

I remained locked up in the town jail the rest of the day. About 11 pm one of the deputies came to my cell. Jim Clark was nearby sleeping off his drunk. He was a heavy drinker. The deputy said: "I'm going to let you go before Sheriff Clark wakes up in a drunken stupor and decides to kill you." — Annie Lee Cooper. [22]

1965 Campaign

In later years, Annie Cooper is elected to the City Council, and today there is an Annie Cooper Avenue in Selma.

Though slugging Clark is a violation of nonviolent discipline, no one in the Freedom Movement holds it against her. Everyone knows Annie Cooper's history of courageous struggle, and behind their impassive faces, everyone on the line is thrilled to see her strike back at the hated sheriff. Most wish they had done it themselves. But the savage retaliation inflicted upon her makes self-evident the tactical necessity of continued nonviolence. And no one can register to vote from a jail cell — if people are going to be arrested it has to be for trying to register. That night the mass meeting is at Tabernacle Baptist. Rev. Anderson praises Annie Cooper, *"Who took a beating today for you and for me."* SCLC leader James Bevel tells the crowd that no matter how justified, retaliatory violence on the part of demonstrators weakens the Movement because, *"Then [the press] don't talk about the registration. We want the world to know they ain't registering nobody!"*

After Dr. King speaks, Rev. Ralph Abernathy comes to the podium. He is an earthy and exuberant speaker. He picks up a police microphone that had been attached to the pulpit after Bevel ordered the police "observers" out of Movement meetings. Calling it a *"doohickey,"* he directly addresses it (and the officials on the other end) to roars of tension-easing laughter:

> Ralph Abernathy isn't afraid of any white man, or any white man's doohicky either. In fact, I'm not afraid to talk to it man to man. Doohickey, hear me well! I want you, doohickey, to tell ... the good white people of Selma that we are not afraid. When we want to have a parade, doohickey, we'll get the R.B. Hudson High School band and take over the town!" He preaches against the evils of segregation to the doohickey and then holds it out toward the audience and challenges, "They have a rumor out that only a few Negroes want to be free. We are all gonna talk to this doohickey tonight! You see, we've got

to let 'em know ... Now before we'll be slaves we'll be what? Talk to the doohickey!" The mass meeting roars its defiance. [7][10]

When the meeting is over, two embarrassed cops remove the doohickey and it is never seen again. But on Tuesday and Wednesday there are more mass arrests at the courthouse as Clark enforces his no-more-than-100 interpretation of the judge's order. Among those arrested are SNCC members John Lewis, Willie Emma Scott, Eugene Rouse, Willie McRae, Stanley Wise, Larry Fox, Joyce Brown, Frank Soracco, and Stokely Carmichael. With the crowds growing larger, Clark calls for reinforcements and Governor Wallace dispatches some 50 Alabama State Troopers under the personal command of Alabama Director of Public Safety "Colonel" Al Lingo. The troopers, and Lingo personally, are notoriously hostile to Blacks and the Freedom Movement. The *Selma Times Journal* reports that in the week since the protests started on January 18 only 40 Blacks have been admitted to the Dallas County courthouse to fill out the voter application and take the literacy test. None have been added to the voter rolls.

Letter from a Selma Jail

ATLANTA: Arrival of the state troopers greatly escalates tension. Meeting with his Executive Staff in Atlanta, Dr. King decides that it's time for him to call attention to the continuing denial of Black voting rights by going to jail in Selma. From his jail cell, he intends to issue a *"Letter from a Selma Jail"* that he hopes will have an effect similar to that of his famous *"Letter from Birmingham Jail."*

Up to now, SCLC senior staff have carefully maneuvered to avoid any risk of King being arrested. Changing that policy is a complex strategic decision. He is the prime symbol of Black resistance to white supremacy and the top target of every racist hate group and fanatic. Clark's deputies are known for their vicious brutality toward Blacks, and past history gives them scant

1965 Campaign

reason to fear any consequences for whatever they might do to a prisoner in their custody. Behind bars, King will be vulnerable to any "lone-gunman" or "crazed assassin" who "mysteriously" finds his way into the Dallas County jail. Moreover, while King is incarcerated, he cannot travel around the country speaking to mass audiences and the national media about the issue of voting rights. Nor can he continue to raise the huge amounts of bail bond money required to keep the Selma campaign going. The Selma marchers are willing to face arrest because they trust that SCLC will bail them out, but if those funds dry up so will the number of protesters.

SELMA: Monday, February 1, is the fifth anniversary of the historic Greensboro Sit-In. Dr. King and Rev. Abernathy lead 260 marchers out of Brown Chapel. Two-by-two they head for the courthouse. As usual, Chief Baker halts the line and orders them to break up into small groups. This time they refuse. As American citizens they have a right to peacefully assemble and march in protest. They know that Baker will arrest them, putting them in the Selma city jail which is run by Baker's police, rather than the county jail which is staffed by Clark's deputies. Most of the marchers are bailed out by SCLC, but as planned, King and Abernathy refuse to post bond and they end up sharing a cell with SCLC staff member Charles Fager. *"This is a deliberate attempt to dramatize conditions in this city, state, and community,"* King tells reporters.

Meanwhile in another church, a throng of students sing freedom songs and wait for the signal. During the January marches, a number of students had simply shown up and participated on their own, but SCLC and SNCC staff made no effort to encourage or mobilize them. Not so today. Organizers have declared February 1st a "Freedom Holiday." After King's mostly adult group is arrested, the students march out more than 500 strong. Some hold cardboard signs with hand-lettered slogans in crayon. All of Baker's cops are herding the first group to jail and processing them through the system, so there's no one to stop the

The Selma Voting Rights Struggle

students. They manage to make it all the way to the courthouse where Clark's deputies bust them, put them on school buses, and take them to the armory where a judge holds a rump court. There they are processed and released to the custody of their parents with a warning never to demonstrate again. But many refuse to cooperate and they are taken to Camp Selma, a state-run, chain-gang-style prison out in the bogs west of the city.

Back at the city jail, arrest fails to intimidate the adult group. While waiting to be booked they drink from the "white" water fountain, switch the "White" and "Colored" signs on the toilets, sing freedom songs, and answer questions with insolence and defiance. Deep in the dingy cell block, King talks quietly with the regular prisoners who tell him their stories of southern injustice. One has been waiting two years for trial with no opportunity for bail. Another was jailed after being beaten by cops on the street. Now 27 months later he has still not been told the charges against him. Others have similar tales. King is saddened, but not surprised. Jails all over the Deep South are the same, and until Blacks gain the vote and enough political power to challenge reigning sheriffs and mayors, nothing is going to change.

PERRY COUNTY: Over in adjacent Perry County, February 1st is their first "Freedom Day." Led by local farmer Albert Turner along with SCLC and SNCC field secretaries James Orange and George Best, 600 people march to the courthouse in Marion (pop. 3,800). Some 115 are allowed inside to fill out the voter application and take the literacy test. Students test the town's white-only businesses for compliance with the Civil Rights Act. Some businesses serve Blacks, others continue to refuse. (Turner, who is the main organizer and head of the Perry County Civil League, later joins the SCLC field staff and eventually becomes SCLC's Alabama Director.)

Students march out of Morning Star Baptist Church in Marion to support voting rights for their parents. A state trooper tells SCLC organizer James Orange, *"Sing one more freedom song and you're under arrest."* The singing continues and 500 are busted. The little county lockup can't hold more than half a dozen prisoners, so they are crammed into a bare concrete stockade and forced to drink from cattle-troughs. After work, some 200 parents assemble at the church and march to protest the brutal conditions inflicted on their children. They too are arrested.

SELMA: The next day, 520 more are sent to jail in Selma, and on Wednesday, another 300 for defying a new injunction issued by Judge Hare forbidding demonstrations outside the courthouse. The total number of arrests in Selma since January 18 is now more than 1,800.

In Selma the cells are full and the small rural lockups are jammed beyond capacity. As arrests mount, prisoners are shuttled to jails and chain-gang camps all over the region. At Camp Selma, the beds are removed so that prisoners have to sleep on the cold concrete floor. They are made to drink from a common tub of water and the single toilet is clogged.

NATIONAL: In New York and Chicago, Friends of SNCC stage sit-ins at federal buildings in support of the Selma campaign and voting rights for Blacks. CORE chapters in the North and West mount similar protests, and hour after hour, pickets circle in front of the White House. From his jail cell, Dr. King issues *"Letter from a Selma Jail."* SCLC publishes it as a full page ad in The New York Times and Freedom Movement supporters circulate it, but it fails to generate the impact of his earlier *"Letter from Birmingham Jail."*

WASHINGTON: President Johnson's attention is focused on Vietnam, not Alabama. For years, "authoritarian regimes" (dictatorships) in South Vietnam have been kept in office by U.S. money and influence. Now, Buddhists are marching in the streets. Some commit self-immolation as desperate acts of protest. Once again, the current military junta is on the verge of collapse. The South Vietnamese army is falling apart — the soldiers don't want to fight — and eight American military "advisors" have just been killed when rebel Viet Cong guerrillas overrun their camp near

The Selma Voting Rights Struggle

Pleiku. The Pentagon is calling for the dispatch of American combat forces and a sustained strategic-bombing campaign against North Vietnam.

Three months earlier, LBJ had campaigned on repeated promises to "Never send American boys to fight in Vietnam," though as the *Pentagon Papers* later reveal, he was already planning to do just that.

The public, however, is taking little note of events in distant Asia. Their attention — and pressure — is focused on Selma, Alabama and LBJ is forced to respond. On Thursday morning, he issues a statement in defense of Black voting rights:

> [All Americans] "should be indignant when one American is denied the right to vote. The loss of that right to a single citizen undermines the freedom of every citizen. This is why all of us should be concerned with the efforts of our fellow Americans to register to vote in Alabama. ... I intend to see that that right is secured for all our citizens." — President Lyndon Johnson. [6]

Meanwhile, under pressure from the Department of Justice and white moderates in Selma who hope that concessions will weaken or divert the movement, Judge Thomas issues a new order on Thursday morning requiring the Dallas County registrars to stop using the literacy test. It also prohibits them from rejecting Blacks for minor spelling errors on their application. He further mandates that they actually *process* at least 100 applications on each of the two days per month that registration is open. This represents a slight improvement over his previous order that merely allowed 100 Blacks to wait in the alley without being arrested. But he does not order that any Blacks actually be added to the voter rolls. Nor does he mandate any increase in the number of registration days. Even if all 100 applicants are added to the rolls on each of those two days per month — which no one believes will happen — that's only 200 per month and there are 15,000 unregistered Blacks in Dallas County. Moreover, his ruling still only applies to this single county and nowhere else in Alabama.

Malcolm X Speaks in Selma

TUSKEGEE: On Wednesday evening, February 3, Malcolm X speaks to the students at Tuskegee Institute. SNCC field secretaries Silas Norman and Fay Bellamy invite him to visit nearby Selma the following day.

SELMA: On Thursday morning, SCLC leaders in Selma abruptly suspend protests while they review and evaluate both the new Thomas ruling and the President's statement. Malcolm arrives at Brown Chapel as students and adults are gathering for the daily march — which has just been canceled. SNCC insists that Malcolm be invited to address the crowd. SCLC leaders and local ministers are opposed. They worry he will condemn nonviolence, incite the young students, laud Islam, disparage Christianity, and alienate white supporters with an anti-white diatribe. All their fears prove completely unfounded.

Malcolm's talk covers a wide range from a history of slavery and racism to internationalism.

> I'm not intending to try and stir you up and make you do something that you wouldn't have done anyway. I pray that God will bless you in everything that you do. I pray that you will grow intellectually, so that you can understand the problems of the world and where you fit into that world picture. And I pray that all the fear that has ever been in your heart will be taken out. — Malcolm X. [7]

Afterward, he briefly speaks to Correta Scott King and Juanita Abernathy who have come to visit their husbands in jail. "Mrs. King, will you tell Dr. King that I had planned to visit with him in jail? I won't get a chance now ... I want Dr. King to know that I didn't come to Selma to make his job difficult. I really did come thinking that I could make it easier. If the white people realize what the alternative is, perhaps they will be more willing to hear Dr. King."

Bound in Jail

SELMA: From his jail cell, Dr. King sends word that suspending protests was a mistake. The next day, Friday, February 5th, the daily marches resume. In the morning, Rev. C.T. Vivian leads some 75 adults to the courthouse. They are all arrested for violating Judge Hare's new injunction prohibiting demonstrations. Some 450 students then march, and they are all arrested too. This brings the total number of voting rights arrests in Dallas and Perry counties to over 3,000. Later that day, King and Abernathy are released on bail.

Most demonstrators, particularly working adults with children to care for and jobs to keep, are quickly bailed out by SCLC. But excessive bail is set for staff organizers and local leaders, and the same is true for students who have been arrested multiple times. Many remain incarcerated for days and then weeks on end. As the cells fill to capacity and overflow, prisoners are transferred to jails in other counties.

Whenever possible, Freedom Movement arrestees are kept segregated from the regular prisoners so as not to contaminate the inmates with dangerous ideas such as speedy-trials, right to an attorney, racially-unbiased justice, and other such "subversive" notions. The main exception to this rule is that white civil rights workers are sometimes locked in with white prisoners who are encouraged by the guards to show these "race traitors" the error of their ways with a thorough beating. For their part, the deputies — all white, of course — inflict their own physical abuse on "uppity" Blacks who are rebelling against the sacred "southern way of life."

Jail food is so foul it's inedible until hunger forces inmates to swallow it down while trying not to gag. Though the authorities allocate a daily budget to feed each prisoner, it's up to the jailers

1965 Campaign

to spend the money as they see fit — and they get to pocket whatever is left over. The result is a salt-encrusted diet of black-eyed peas or lima beans contaminated by roaches, a square of crumbly cornbread, acrid black coffee, and on special occasions, grits or a boiled chicken neck. But small as the expenditures are, as the number of prisoners swells, so too do the costs of feeding and guarding them, thereby diminishing the "surplus" funds that deputies and guards are accustomed to skimming off the top.

Inside the jammed cells, Movement prisoners endure uncertainty, boredom, rats, roaches, clogged toilets, inedible food, lack of showers, sweltering heat, and freezing cold. Freedom songs and spontaneous group prayer bolster their courage and spirit. When not singing or praying there is talk. The boys talk about girls (and sex), and the girls talk about boys (and sex). There are also ongoing discussions and debates about the Movement, strategy, tactics, nonviolence, Black history, economics, civics, politics, philosophy, and a universe of other subjects. Some of the prisoners are college graduates or undergrads, some are still in segregated "Colored" schools where many topics are forbidden and cannot be spoken of openly, and some have had little or no formal education at all, though they are well-schooled in the brutal realities of white supremacy and Black exploitation. Each person teaches what they know, and soaks up new knowledge from everyone else. The jam-packed cells become intellectual pressure-cookers where new ideas, new concepts, and new contexts ferment, bubble and fume. In later years, some of the young students tell interviewers that it was this jailhouse university that inspired them to find their way to college, something they had not previously thought might apply to themselves.

Sometimes, as the tension and frustration grow intolerable, there are arguments and bitter recriminations. There are also jokes and japes and jeers and laughter. One perennial favorite is that sooner or later someone newly arrested and shoved into a crowded cell inevitably asks, *"How long do you think we'll be in here?"*

The Selma Voting Rights Struggle

A veteran of the cage replies, *"What did you say your name was, again?"*

When the new fish answers, the old hand nods wisely and says, *"Oh, yeah, you're on the B-list."*

"The B-list? What's the B-list?"

And everyone then shouts, *"You're going to beeeeee here for a looooong time!"*

Clubs and Cattle Prods

MONTGOMERY: Courthouse marches and arrests continue in Selma, but an effort to expand the campaign into Montgomery fizzles. Only a hundred potential voters show up for a march to the Montgomery courthouse. When they arrive, officials open the books and allow them to apply without hindrance. There is no drama, no tension, and no follow up.

WASHINGTON: On Tuesday, February 9, Dr. King travels to Washington to meet with Attorney General Nicholas Katzenbach, Vice President Hubert Humphrey, and briefly with President Johnson. LBJ is still preoccupied with Vietnam, but the Selma campaign is generating intense public and congressional pressure to do something about Black voting rights. He tells King that he will soon send legislation addressing the issue to Congress — though what it will consist of is not clear.

SELMA: Sacrifice and suffering are beginning to wear down the Black community. Some are becoming discouraged and weary after weeks of futile struggle. Adults and children are enduring arrest after arrest and longer sojourns in dreary cells, parents are being fired from jobs and families evicted from their shacks. The weather is wet and cold and, in too many homes, there's scant funds for food and even less for heat. And no one is being registered to vote. No one is being registered to vote, no victories are in sight, not even small ones such as a neighbor or relative achieving recognition as a citizen-voter.

1965 Campaign

On the white side, the costs of policing marches, arresting thousands of demonstrators, and feeding, guarding, and transporting hundreds of prisoners is bankrupting Dallas County. Deputies and jailors are personally feeling the effects as they're forced to spend money on feeding prisoners that normally would find its way into their personal pockets as traditional perks of office. They are not amused.

On Wednesday, February 10, some 160 students march to the courthouse carrying hand-lettered signs reading "Let Our Parents Vote," "Wallace Must Go," and "Jim Clark is a Cracker." By now, the courthouse protests have become routine; everyone knows what to expect, and with so many of the SCLC and SNCC staff either in jail or working in the outlying counties, the students are organizing and leading their own marches. But this time is different.

"Move out!" Clark shouts, and his deputies and possemen herd the students — some as young as nine — down Alabama Avenue toward the jail. They assume they're being arrested as usual. But instead of entering the jail, the cops force them to start running. *"You wanted to march, didn't you? March, dammit, march!"* shout the deputies as they jab and poke with their clubs. Clark rides along in his car as the young protesters are forced to run down Water Street and then out on lonely, isolated River Road bordering the Alabama River sloughs and bogs. Clubs strike those not moving fast enough and the searing pain of the possemen's electric cattle-prods burn through their winter clothes. Run! Run! Faster! Faster!

At the creek bridge, sheriffs use their cars to block the road so that reporters and photographers back at the courthouse — who were taken by surprise by Clark's switch — cannot catch up. A fifteen-year-old boy pants to a guard, *"God sees you."* The deputy smashes him in the mouth with his hardwood club. Some of the students collapse, vomiting, and shaking. They are beaten with clubs to keep them moving until they can run no more. Some bolt, or are driven, into the bogs, others manage to escape to a Black-owned farm.

The Selma Voting Rights Struggle

Clark returns to the courthouse. With a smirk and wink, he tells reporters that the student prisoners "escaped" his custody. SNCC Chairman John Lewis writes out a statement on a scrap of paper:

> This is one more example of the inhuman, animal-like treatment of the Negro people of Selma, Alabama. This nation has always come to the aid of people in foreign lands who are gripped by a reign of tyranny. Can this nation do less for the people of Selma? — John Lewis. [11]

Clark's brutal treatment of the Black community's children re-energizes the movement which had been sagging under the weight of march after march, arrest after arrest, all for little result. The next day, Thursday, more than 400 adults and students march to the courthouse in a revitalized show of strength. The wave of adverse publicity caused by Clark's cruelty temporarily gives Wilson Baker the upper hand in the ongoing struggle between them, so Baker is able to apply his "kill 'em with kindness" strategy. Hare's injunction is not enforced, and no one is arrested or beaten. Clark and Hare are furious.

Holding On and Pushing Forward

Arrests continue to mount, people continue to lose their jobs, and the endurance of Selma's Black community is sorely tested. Tension and disagreement among SCLC, SNCC, and DCVL leaders erupt into dispute. The immediate issue is how to respond to the minimal concessions contained in Judge Thomas order of February 4th, a question that invokes the conflict between SCLC's goal of winning national legislation, SNCC's dedication to grassroots community organizing of those at the bottom of society, and DCVL's focus on matters specific to Selma and Dallas County. Initially, SCLC and SNCC reject the order and boycott its procedures, most notably an "appearance book" that Blacks may sign whenever they wish. Under the new Thomas ruling, on the two days per month the Registration office is open Blacks will be allowed to fill out the voter application in the order

1965 Campaign

their names are listed in the appearance book — without having to wait all day in the alley. But as SNCC organizers Silas Norman and John Love report:

> SNCC staff in Selma disagreed basically with the requirement that Negroes should be made to sign an appearance book in order to be processed, as this was just one more form of discrimination. Sheriff Clark has made a mockery of this court order by calling off the numbers which the people were given when they signed the appearance book so fast that people can't possibly get from their place in line to the registrar's office in time to be registered. Sheriff Clark may keep doing this; we don't know. — Silas Norman and John Love. [12]

DCVL argues that even though the Thomas order does not apply to any other county in the state, it should be characterized as a small, encouraging, partial victory to raise spirits. And its procedures should be followed in the hope of getting at least some Black voters added to the rolls. With the national press hammering the Movement for rejecting Thomas' token measures — *"Negroes Don't Know What They Want"* claims the Associated Press (AP) — SCLC fears that such stories will derail chances for national legislation, so SCLC leaders reverse their position on boycotting the appearance book. SNCC continues to oppose the new procedures because they apply only to Blacks and offer no hope of illiterate Blacks ever being registered because the order only requires that they be "processed," not that they be registered. In the end, a decision is made to suspend the appearance book boycott, mobilize Selma Blacks to sign it, and concentrate more heavily on the rural counties where the order does not apply.

Meanwhile, SCLC leader James Bevel is incarcerated in the sheriff's county jail where he is the target of unremitting abuse and degradation. Word filters out that he has fallen seriously ill with viral pneumonia and the deputies are hosing him down with cold water in an unheated cell. His wife, Diane Nash Bevel, works the phones calling reporters and federal officials about his desperate condition. Finally, she manages to get him transferred to an infirmary where he is shackled with iron chains to a bed until she is able to get them removed.

On Monday, February 15, voter registration offices are open for applications. This is the second and last voter registration day in February. The local white power structure is still reeling from the bad publicity of Clark's brutal forced march. For the moment, Mayor Smitherman and Baker have the upper hand in their political conflict with the Hare-Clark faction. Baker grants a parade permit so that Blacks can march to the courthouse. Assured there will be no arrests or police violence, some 1,500 Black men and women march in the largest protest to date.

Though the marchers are hopeful there will be no arrests or beatings, they all know they are risking economic retaliation. Some are taking an unauthorized day off work and the consequences could be termination. Others risk evictions, foreclosures, and business boycotts. For many, it is their first march. Later, Sheyann Webb recalled:

> "What time they marchin'?" my daddy asked. It was so strange the way he said it, and I knew that he and Momma were going to go that day. ... I hugged them both. I was so proud of them. It was late in the morning — maybe ten-thirty or so — when the march started. ... I walked between my parents, holding their hands, and we sang all the way down there. But the jubilation soon began to diminish as we stood and stood. The line moved at a crawl. At noon, some of the courthouse workers came out, and I remember some white women going by and spraying Raid insecticide and another can of some kind of disinfectant toward us; they wrinkled up their noses like we were smelly things. I remember my momma's eyes got wide and her mouth was set in a tight line, like she wanted to shout at them, but some of the

1965 Campaign

march leaders were walking up and down the line telling us to stay calm. So we started singing again.

We stayed there until late in the afternoon, and when Momma and Daddy got in they were told they couldn't be registered that day but were given a number which, they were told by the man in the office, would "hold" their place the next registration day. It was a disappointment to all of us. But as we hurried home Momma was saying she didn't care how long it took, she was going to be back each day they held registration until she could vote. She was now determined. ... And when I say we hurried home, I mean it. Standing there all day was not only a challenge of our resolve to be full citizens, but also was an endurance test of our bladders. — Sheyann Webb. [9]

The line of waiting applicants stretches for blocks in the dank February cold. Over the course of the day, almost 100 who have low numbers in the appearance book are allowed to fill out voter applications, some 600 more sign the book for a chance to apply in the future. When school ends in the afternoon, the teachers join the end of the queue, and 800 students march by to honor the adults.

The Selma Voting Rights Struggle

WILCOX COUNTY: That same day, in adjacent Wilcox County — about as rural as an Alabama county can get — Dr. King accompanies 70 Blacks to the courthouse in Camden. Some are allowed to fill out the application and take the literacy test, but even in the unlikely event they pass the test, they cannot be registered because there are no registered Black voters to "vouch" for them and no white voter would dare do so.

Wilcox County, Alabama Voter Registration 1961

Whites Over 21	2,634	30%
Registered White Voters	2,950	*112%
Blacks Over 21	6,085	70%
Registered Black Voters	0	0%

* White registration exceeds 100% because whites are retained on the voting rolls after they die or move away. Oddly, these dead or gone "tombstone" voters often manage to cast votes for the incumbents in every election.

PERRY COUNTY: King leaves Camden and drives to Perry County where another long line of Blacks is waiting at the courthouse in Marion for a chance to register. When the registration office closes at the end of the day, 150 are still waiting. The cops drive them off with clubs.

Perry County, Alabama Voter Registration 1961

Whites Over 21	3,441	40%
Registered White Voters	3,235	94%
Blacks Over 21	5,202	60%
Registered Black Voters	265	5%

1965 Campaign

LOWNDES COUNTY: In Lowndes, which adjoins Dallas County on the east, Blacks comprise 80% of the population but no Blacks have voted there since the end of Reconstruction. Freedom Movement activists hope to develop a registration campaign, but the Klan is so strong in "Bloody Lowndes" and white violence so prevalent, that no Black church dares the risk of holding a meeting. That's just fine by Carl Golson, the Lowndes County Registrar of Voters, who tells a reporter, *"I don't know of any Negro registrations here, but there is a better relationship between the whites and the niggers here than any place I know of."*

Lowndes County, Alabama Voter Registration 1961

Whites Over 21	1,900	27%
Registered White Voters	2,240	*118%
Blacks Over 21	5,122	73%
Registered Black Voters	0	0%

* As in Wilcox County, white voter registration exceeds their numbers in the population of Lowndes County. Dead or absent 'voters' likely cast ballots for the incumbents.

SELMA: Later that evening, the turnout for the nightly mass meeting at Brown Chapel is large. Large and frustrated. Despite marches, arrests, court orders, and over a thousand appearance book signatures, only a trickle of Blacks have been registered to vote. Hosea Williams tells them that despite the huge number of Blacks who lined up at the courthouse that day, *"We're just about as far from freedom tonight as we were last night."*

The Selma Voting Rights Struggle

The Shooting of Jimmy Lee Jackson

SELMA: The sight of 1,500 Blacks freely marching to the courthouse in Selma without arrest or retribution outrages Hare, Clark, and the other hard-line segregationists. The White Citizens Council runs a full-page ad in the Selma Times-Journal equating the Civil Rights Act with Communism, and in a sign that the political tide is swinging back toward Hare and Clark, the paper editorializes that King has pushed *"... all sound-thinking citizens perilously near the breaking point."*

PERRY COUNTY: At a meeting in adjacent Perry County, angry whites physically attack two of their own for daring to suggest negotiating with Blacks, and local officials ask Governor Wallace to send them a force of state troopers to bolster their small sheriffs department which doesn't have enough deputies, or any organized posse, to suppress rising Black discontent.

SELMA: The focus is now on adding new signatures to the appearance book rather than lining up *en masse* day after day at the Dallas County courthouse. On Tuesday, February 16th, John Lewis of SNCC and C.T. Vivian of SCLC lead a small band of those who have not yet signed the book to add their names. Both men are stalwarts of the Freedom Movement having come up together through the Nashville sit-ins, Freedom Rides, Parchman Prison, Albany, Birmingham, and Freedom Summer in Mississippi. A cold rain is falling as Vivian leads the little group to the Alabama Street entrance where an overhang provides some shelter. Sheriff Clark bars the door, allowing only a few at a time inside. Citing Judge Hare's injunction, Clark orders the remainder to leave. C.T. confronts him face to face, *"You're a racist the same way Hitler was a racist!"* Deputies push them off the steps with their clubs, knocking several people to the pavement. Vivian leads them back to the door. They demand to be let in out of the rain. A deputy smashes his fist into C.T's face, sending him reeling back with blood flowing from his mouth. And then, they drag him off to jail.

1965 Campaign

At the mass meeting on Wednesday night, DCVL leader Rev. Reese calls for an economic boycott of white stores owned by, or employing, members of Clark's posse. Dr. King, ill with a viral fever, hoarsely tells the crowd, *"Selma still isn't right! ... It may well be we might have to march out of this church at night..."*

By now, most of those in Brown Chapel are veterans of direct action and they are grimly aware of what a night march implies. Night marches allow adults with jobs to participate after work, a factor that increases numbers and political impact. But night marches are dangerous because Klansmen, police, and possemen can attack under cover of darkness with little risk of being identified. Even with flash bulbs and portable spotlights, the range of media cameras is sharply curtailed. It's easy for the cops to keep reporters far enough away so that nothing is recorded on film.

PERRY COUNTY: The next day, Thursday, the 18th of February, twenty carloads of Alabama State Troopers led by Al Lingo swarm into Marion to suppress Black defiance and restore peaceful tranquility to the "southern way of life." SCLC project director James Orange is spotted walking on the street and is arrested for "contributing to the delinquency of minors" (by encouraging students to march around the courthouse singing freedom songs).

James Orange is immensely popular among both young and old in Perry County's Black community, and that night tiny Zion Methodist Church is packed to overflowing as word spreads of his arrest. The lockup where Orange is being held is just a block and a half away. The plan is for a short night march so they can sing freedom songs outside his cell window and then return. If the troopers block them, they plan to kneel in prayer and then go back to the church.

Albert Turner and local minister, Rev. James Dobynes, lead 400 marchers out of the church and up Pickens Street two-by-two on the sidewalk. They are halted by Lingo's troopers. Jim Clark and

The Selma Voting Rights Struggle

some of his Selma posse are also present, along with an angry mob of local whites. As planned, Dobynes kneels and begins to pray. Suddenly, all the streetlights go dark. The mob savagely attacks news reporters covering the protest. Richard Valeriani of NBC is clubbed, his head bloodied. Some of the mob have come prepared with cans of spray paint they use to sabotage camera lenses. Others smash the TV lights. No photos are taken of the troopers, deputies, and possemen wading into the line of marchers with hardwood clubs and ax-handles flailing, beating men, women, and children to the ground. Rev Dobynes is struck down and they continue to beat him as he's dragged off to the nearby jail. The pavement literally runs red with blood.

Marchers desperately try to retreat to the church, but many are cut off. Some of the fleeing marchers take refuge in Mack's Cafe, a small Black-owned jook joint. Among them are Cager Lee, 82, his daughter Viola Jackson, and her son, military veteran and church deacon, Jimmie Lee Jackson, 26, tried to register to vote five times and each time has been denied. Troopers follow them in, smashing out the lights, overturning tables, and beating people indiscriminately. They attack Cager in the kitchen. His daughter tries to come to his aid and they knock her to the floor. Jimmie tries to protect his mother, and one trooper throws him up against the cigarette machine while another shoots him twice, point-blank in the stomach. They club him repeatedly, driving him out into the street where he collapses.

SCLC field secretary Willie Bolden recalls:

> After the speeches, we decided to have a short march to the courthouse to protest the arrest of our co-worker, James Orange. We filed out, and turned toward the courthouse. The cameras were shooting. All of a sudden we heard cameras being broken and newsmen being hit. I saw people running out of the church. ... The troopers were in there beating folks while local police were outside beating anyone who came out the door. ... A big white fella came up to me and stuck a double-barreled

1965 Campaign

shotgun, cocked, in my stomach. "You're the nigger from Atlanta, aren't you? Somebody wants to see you," he said, and he took me across the street to this guy with a badge and red suspenders and chewing tobacco. "See what you caused," he said, and he spun me around, "I want you to watch this." There were people running over each other and trying to protect themselves.

One guy was running toward us. When he saw the cops he tried to make a U-turn and he ran into a local cop. They just hit him in the head and bust his head wide open. Blood spewed all over and he fell. When I tried to go to him, the sheriff pulled me back and stuck a .38 snubnose in my mouth. He cocked the hammer back and said, "What I really need to do is blow your God damned brains out, nigger." ... I was scared to death! He said, "Take this nigger to jail." So they took me, and they hit me all over the arms and legs and thighs and chin. There were others there got beaten the same. ... There were literally puddles of blood leading all the way up the stairs to the jail cell. ... Shortly after I was in there we heard the shots. That's when Jimmy Lee Jackson got killed. They cops were beating on his mama, and he was headed toward his mother and that's when they shot him. — Willie Bolden. [13][15]

A reporter encounters Jim Clark prowling the streets with some of his possemen. When asked why he's in Marion, Clark replies, *"Things got a little too quiet for me over in Selma tonight. It made me nervous."*

Perry County has no hospital and the local infirmary is swamped with serious injuries. An unknown number of others lie wounded in jail. The infirmary is not equipped to care for gunshot wounds, so Jimmie Lee Jackson is rushed 30 miles by ambulance to Selma in adjacent Dallas County. Since the "white" public hospital there won't treat Black protesters, he's brought to the Catholic-run Good Samaritan Hospital.

Tension Escalates

NEW YORK: On Sunday evening, February 21, 1965, Malcolm X is assassinated in Harlem under circumstances that remain controversial. His death hits the Civil Rights Movement hard. Despite tactical differences over integration and nonviolence, he is seen as a courageous and forthright Black leader in the fight against white supremacy. John Lewis attends his funeral and later says: *"I had my differences with him, of course, but there was no question that he had come to articulate better than anyone else on the scene — including Dr. King — the bitterness and frustration of Black Americans."* [11]

ALABAMA: Governor Wallace issues an unconstitutional order barring all night-time marches everywhere in the state and assigns 75 troopers under Lingo to enforce his version of "law and order" in Selma. At a rally of the Dallas County White Citizens Council, former Mississippi Governor Ross Barnett tells some 2,000 whites that they face, *"... absolute extinction of all we hold dear unless we are victorious."* After the shooting of Jimmie Lee Jackson and the murder of Malcolm X, hope begins to waver, and the mood of Alabama Blacks turns increasingly bleak.

SELMA: Day after day, vigils for Jimmie Lee Jackson are held outside Good Samaritan, and mass meetings in Black churches around the state condemn the shooting and pray for his recovery. Despite their anguish and sorrow, grimly determined groups continue marching to the Dallas County courthouse in Selma to add their names to the appearance book. DCVL leader Amelia Boynton calls on Blacks to expand the economic boycott to all white-owned businesses as well as the city buses that still require Blacks to sit at the rear.

Selma is the main commercial center for Dallas County. Portions of Wilcox, Perry, Marengo, and Lowndes counties all have Black majorities. Every Saturday, the white-owned stores in the segregated Black shopping district east of Broad Street teem with rural Blacks making their weekly purchases. The customers are

1965 Campaign

all Black. Except for an occasional janitor or scrub-woman, the employees are all white.

BLACK BELT: James Orange, now out of jail, expands the campaign into Hale County to the north of Perry; other organizers begin working Marengo County to the west of Dallas. And over in "Bloody Lowndes" to the east, where no Black in living memory has been registered to vote, James Bevel, now out of the hospital, tries to stealthily infiltrate, *"like Caleb and Joshua,"* seeking — without success — a church that will host a voting rights meeting.

LOWNDES COUNTY: Every fourth Sunday, Rev. Lorenzo Harrison of Selma preaches to tiny Mount Carmel Baptist Church in Lowndes County a few miles from Hayneville, the county seat. Word of Bevel's effort leaks back to the white power structure and a rumor spreads among whites that Harrison intends to speak about Black voting rights. Carloads of Klansmen armed with rifles and shotguns surround the church. Members of the little congregation recognize Tom Coleman, son of the sheriff and an unpaid "special deputy," who in 1959 was known to have murdered Richard Lee Jones at a chain-gang prison camp. (Soon he will kill again.) Another is a plantation owner with 10,000 acres who had once shot to death a Black sharecropper because he seemed too happy at the prospect of being drafted out of the fields and into the Army. Mount Carmel Church has no phone they can use to call for help — few Blacks in Lowndes have telephone service and those that do suspect their calls are monitored and reported to authorities. With quiet courage, Deacon John Hulett manages to smuggle Harrison to safety. (Five years later, in 1970, Black voters elect John Hulett sheriff.)

SELMA: On Tuesday the 23rd, Al Lingo serves an arrest warrant for "assault and battery" on Jackson whose life is slowly fading as infection saps his strength. On Friday morning, February 26, Jimmie Lee Jackson dies.

In 2007 — 42 years later — former Alabama State Trooper James

The Selma Voting Rights Struggle

Fowler is indicted for Jackson's murder. In 2010, he pleads guilty to manslaughter and is sentenced to six months in jail. None of the other white law enforcement officials involved face charges for the police-mob violence in Marion.

PERRY COUNTY: Voter registration offices will be open again on Monday, March 1, and over the weekend SCLC and SNCC organizers concentrate on mobilizing Blacks in Dallas, Perry, Wilcox, Marengo, and Hale counties to honor Jimmie Lee Jackson and demand their right to vote. At a Sunday memorial service and voter registration rally in Marion, James Bevel preaches from the Book of Esther and tells the congregation: *"We must go to Montgomery and see the king! Be prepared to walk to Montgomery! Be prepared to sleep on the highway!"* By this, he means not a march *in* Montgomery, but a march *on* the state capitol to present to Governor Wallace a demand for justice in the murder of Jimmy Lee Jackson and also their call for voting rights. Old Cager Lee and Jimmie Lee's mother, Viola Jackson, bandages still covering their injuries, are ready to join him.

BLACK BELT: On Monday a cold rain drenches the Alabama Black Belt, discouraging turnout and chilling to the bone those who are forced to wait outside their courthouses for a chance to fill out voter applications — 300 in Selma, 200 in Wilcox, hundreds in Perry, and, for the first time, small groups in Hale, Marengo and Lowndes counties.

LOWNDES COUNTY: Led by John Hulett, a small band of 30 or so show up at the courthouse in Hayneville to apply for the vote. They are told by Registrar Carl Golson that voting applications are taken at a location two miles down the road. A dozen of them walk through pouring rain only to be told that no, it's the courthouse where you register to vote. When they finally make it back to Hayneville, Golson tells them that it's too late, the office is now closed though it's still early afternoon. Driving from county to county to encourage the effort, Dr. King arrives and tries to speak to Golson who refuses. Wet, chilled, and dejected, the twelve return to their homes.

1965 Campaign

SELMA and MARION: The rain is still coming down on Wednesday, the day of Jimmie Lee Jackson's funeral. In Selma, R.B. Hudson High is nearly empty as the students boycott class for his memorial service. Two thousand mourners file past the coffin in Brown Chapel where a banner reads, "Racism killed our brother." In Marion, where 400 manage to jam themselves inside Zion church for Jackson's service and 600 wait outside in the rain, Dr. King asks: *"Who killed him?"*

> He was murdered by the brutality of every sheriff who practiced lawlessness in the name of law. He was murdered by the irresponsibility of every politician from governors on down who has fed his constituents the stale bread of hatred and the spoiled meat of racism. He was murdered by the timidity of a federal government that is willing to spend millions of dollars a day to defend freedom in Vietnam but cannot protect the rights of its citizens at home. ... And he was murdered by the cowardice of every Negro who passively accepts the evils of segregation and stands on the sidelines in the struggle for justice. — Martin Luther King. [10]

Walking slowly in the rain, the funeral cortege that follows the hearse to the burial site is half a mile long.

WASHINGTON: In the two months since the voting rights campaign began with the January 2nd mass meeting in Brown Chapel, there have been more than 4,000 arrests in the Black Belt of Alabama. But hardly more than a handful of new Black voters have been registered. In Washington, public and Congressional pressure to do something is intensifying. Adding to that pressure is Soviet propaganda, international condemnation, and the realities of Cold War geopolitics. Reluctantly, grudgingly, the White House and Justice Department begin to consider what role (if any) the national government might play in securing voting rights for Blacks and other racial minorities.

The Selma Voting Rights Struggle

ATLANTA: Dr. King endorses Bevel's proposal for a march from Selma to Montgomery. But SNCC opposes the SCLC plan. They see it as a dangerous grandstand play by King that will do nothing for the local people. John Lewis disagrees, "I knew the feelings that were out there on the streets. The people of Selma were hurting. They were angry. They needed to march. It didn't matter to me who led it. They needed to march."

Lewis stands alone and is outvoted. The SNCC meeting does agree that SNCC members can participate in the march as individuals, but not as SNCC representatives. SNCC sends a letter to King stating: "*We strongly believe that the objectives of the march do not justify the dangers ... consequently [SNCC] will only live up to those minimal commitments ... to provide radios and cars, ... and nothing beyond that.*" [11]

MONTGOMERY: Declaring that the march is "*Not conducive to the orderly flow of traffic and commerce,*" Governor Wallace issues an edict forbidding it. "*[The] march cannot and will not be tolerated.*" He orders the state troopers to "*Use whatever measures are necessary to prevent a march.*"

SELMA: On Friday the 5th, Hosea Williams asks the Medical Committee for Human Rights (MCHR) for doctors and nurses in case of violence. Led by Dr. Al Moldovan, six MCHR doctors and three nurses arrive Saturday in Selma. The march is scheduled to leave Selma on Sunday, March 7th.

Anticipating that their march will not be allowed out of Selma, SCLC leaders make few logistic preparations for a 50-mile trek to Montgomery over four or five days. They assume everyone will be arrested for violating Wallace's edict. The plan is to kneel and pray when ordered to turn around or disperse. By refilling the jails, they will maintain pressure on Washington and the federal courts. Though he had previously said he would lead the march, SCLC leaders convince King to remain in Atlanta — he is more valuable out of jail speaking and mobilizing support than sitting in a cell. It's a decision that infuriates SNCC field workers in

1965 Campaign

Selma who condemn it as a betrayal of the local marchers (though they themselves are still refusing to participate in the march).

On Saturday, March 6th, a new kind of civil rights march — a white march — takes place in Selma. Led by Rev. Joseph Ellwanger, of Birmingham, 70 members of Concerned White Citizens of Alabama assemble from all over the state at the Dallas County courthouse in support of Black voting rights. Largely organized by women from the Alabama Human Relations Council, they are mostly college professors, ministers, Unitarians, researchers from the Huntsville rocket lab, and their wives. They are not the only outsiders coming into Selma — Klansmen and other arch-segregationists armed with ax handles, iron pipes and steel chains have been drawn by anticipation of a violent confrontation with marching Blacks on the morrow. Along with some of Clark's possemen, they harass and menace the pro-civil rights whites. Just before violence breaks out, Selma Police Chief Wilson Baker manages to extricate Ellwanger's group to safety.

chapter 3

The March to Montgomery

March 7, "Bloody Sunday"

SELMA: Sunday, March 7th, dawns cold and raw. Tension grips the city. The air is pregnant with potential violence. Carloads of white thugs prowl the streets looking for trouble. Just over the Edmund Pettus Bridge on the road to Montgomery, a swarm of state troopers, sheriff's deputies and mounted possemen, wait impatiently, itching for action. John Carter Lewis, a Black dishwasher, is stopped on his way home from work. He's guilty of being Black in the wrong place. Two troopers attack him, striking him with their clubs, breaking his arm and bloodying his head.

After divine worship, some 400 marchers gather at Brown Chapel. Some are still in their Sunday suits and dresses; others carry knapsacks and rolled-up blankets tied with rough twine. Their mood is somber but determined. There is little of the spirited singing that buoyed previous protests.

The Selma Voting Rights Struggle

> We expected a confrontation. We knew that Sheriff Clark had issued yet another call the evening before for even more deputies. Mass arrests would probably be made. There might be injuries. Most likely, we would be stopped at the edge of the city limits, arrested, and maybe roughed up a little bit. We did not expect anything worse than that. — John Lewis. [11]

The MCHR medical team sets up a first aid station at Brown Chapel — a table, a mattress, and some basic medical supplies.

> Even though we had been demonstrating for two years now, we had the uneasiness that this was going to be a different day — uneasiness is to put it mildly, if not euphemistically, because frankly it was a fear, it was a terror that was going through us all. We were scared, because we didn't know what was going to happen. — Charles Bonner, Selma student leader. [14]

With horns blaring, a caravan of cars, filled with 200 marchers from Perry County, rolls in and unloads. Off to the side, SCLC divides its field workers into two groups, those who will march and presumably end up in jail, and those who will stay behind to mobilize a follow-on protest. James Bevel, Andrew Young, and Hosea Williams flip coins to decide who will lead the march in King's absence. Hosea is the odd man out.

It is mid-afternoon when the 600 or so marchers line up two-by-two and head for the bridge. Leading the line are Hosea Williams and John Lewis; behind them are SCLC leader Albert Turner of Marion and Bob Mants of SNCC. (It is SNCC policy that no one is allowed to go into danger alone, so he volunteers to accompany John despite SNCC's opposition to the march.) A few rows behind them are two of Selma's indomitable leaders, Amelia Boynton and Marie Foster. A handful of white civil rights workers and Movement supporters are mixed in among the Black students, teachers, maids, laborers, and farmers who make up most of the marchers. Behind them is a flatbed truck with some

The March to Montgomery

rented portable toilets and a few ambulances staffed by MCHR medics. (Except for one ambulance, all are hearses owned by Black funeral parlors.)

Police roadblocks have closed the bridge to vehicles. The MCHR ambulances are blocked. Gangs of possemen on foot lurk nearby. The marchers remain on the sidewalk as they start up the bridge rise. When the leaders reach the crest, they see what awaits them on the other side. State trooper cars, their lights flashing, are parked across the highway. A phalanx of more than 200 troopers and sheriff's deputies are lined up two and three deep to bar the march. To one side is a band of possemen in their khaki uniforms and construction helmets. More than a dozen of them are mounted on horses and they carry long leather bullwhips. White thugs armed with bats and pipes and waving Confederate battle flags crowd the burger-joint parking lot.

As the marchers start down the bridge slope toward the waiting cops, Hosea Williams looks over the rail at the cold, choppy waters of the Alabama River 100 feet below. *"Can you swim?"* he asks John Lewis.

"No."

"Neither can I, but we might have to."

The media is confined off to the side where their view is limited. With their usual clueless certainty, TV reporters are telling viewers that the "militant" SNCC has "forced" this dangerous march on an "unwilling" Dr. King.

> We kept stepping two by two, one foot in front of the other one, marching resolutely into hell, because it was so clear that we were going to be beaten. I mean, these men were just so prepared, they were not going to let their readiness go to waste by not beating us. I mean, when you look back on it, it was very clear. — Charles Bonner. [14]

The Selma Voting Rights Struggle

When they come down off the bridge, the marchers cross over the Selma city line into the county jurisdiction of Sheriff Clark. The troopers and deputies begin donning their gas masks. The marchers stride forward on the shoulder of US 80, known in Alabama as the Jefferson Davis Highway. The front of the line is about 100 feet from the bridge when Major Cloud of the state troopers orders Williams and Lewis to halt and turn around. As planned, the leaders motion for everyone to kneel in prayer.

"Troopers Advance!" shouts the Major. A wave of cops smashes into the people at the front of the line.

> Williams and Lewis stumbled backward into the pair behind them and went down, with troopers in turn falling on top of them. As the column dissolved in panic, the troopers broke ranks and began running after the Blacks, clubs swinging wildly. ... One after another of them was knocked to the pavement, screaming in pain and terror, the wooden clubs thudding into their flesh. From the sidelines a shrill cheer went up from the watching whites. — Charles Fager. [10]

> The troopers and possemen swept forward as one, like a human wave, a blur of blue shirts and billy clubs and bullwhips. We had no chance to turn and retreat. There were six hundred people behind us, bridge railings to either side and the river below. ... The first of the troopers came over me, a large husky man. Without a word he swung his club against the left side of my head. I didn't feel any pain, just the thud of the blow, and my legs giving way. ... And then the same trooper hit me again. And everything started to spin. I heard something that sounded like gunshots. And then a cloud of smoke rose all around us. Tear gas. ... I began choking, coughing. I couldn't get air into my lungs. I felt as if I was taking my last breath. — John Lewis. [11]

The March to Montgomery

> From between nearby buildings a line of horses emerged at the gallop, their riders wearing the possemen's irregular uniform and armed with bullwhips, ropes, and lengths of rubber tubing wrapped with barbed wire. They rode into the melee with wild rebel yells, while behind them the cheers of the spectators grew even louder. "Get those Goddamned niggers!" came Jim Clark's voice. "And get those Goddamned white niggers!" — Charles Fager. [10]

Amelia Boynton is viciously clubbed to the ground and tear gas is shot directly into her face as she collapses into unconsciousness. Hosea Williams scoops up little Sheyann Webb and carries her to safety through the tear gas and charging horses.

> He held on until we were off the bridge and down on Broad Street and he let me go. I didn't stop running until I got home. ... I was maybe a little hysterical because I kept repeating over and over, "I can't stop shaking Momma, I can't stop shaking." ... My daddy was like I'd never seen him before. He had a shotgun and he yelled, "By God, if they want it this way, I'll give it to them!" And he started out the door. Momma jumped up and got in front of him. ... Finally he put the gun aside and sat down. I remember just laying there on the couch, crying and feeling so disgusted. They had beaten us like we were slaves. — Sheyann Webb. [9]

Behind the possemen come the white thugs, beating down anyone who manages to stumble out of the gas cloud. They assault the reporters and break their cameras. One of the "reporters" is actually an FBI agent, and the three men who attack him are later arrested for assault on a federal agent. They are the only whites ever arrested for violence on "Bloody Sunday" but are never brought to trial.

The Selma Voting Rights Struggle

The troopers, deputies, possemen, and thugs pursue the retreating marchers over the bridge and through the city streets, beating and assaulting Blacks wherever they find them — whether they're demonstrators or not. Dr. Moldovan and nurses Virginia Wells and Linda Dugan plunge into the swirling tumult. They lift unconscious and crippled victims into their ambulance and race back to the aid station at Brown Chapel, which is quickly swamped with the injured and wounded. By the end of the day, 100 of the 600 marchers require medical attention for fractured skulls, broken teeth and limbs, gas poisoning, and whip lashes.

The troopers and possemen swarm into the Carver Project beating whomever they catch and charging their horses up the steps of Brown Chapel to attack those trying to seek sanctuary in the church. Another band of possemen force their way into First Baptist and throw a teenage boy through stained a glass window. Sheriff Clark fires tear gas into homes to drive people outside where they can be attacked. Baker tries to stop the carnage, but Clark shouts in his face, *"I've already waited a month too damn long!"*

Sheyann Webb's constant companion, Rachel West, 8 years old, recalls:

> I saw the horsemen ... riding at a gallop, coming around a house up the way, and that's when I turned and ran. I heard the horses' hooves and I turned and saw the riders hitting at the people and they were coming fast toward me. I stopped and got up against the wall of one of the apartment buildings and pressed myself against it as hard as I could. Two horsemen went by and I knew if I didn't move I would be trapped there. I saw the people crying [from the gas] as they went by and holding their eyes and some had their arms up over their heads.
>
> I took off running. ... I was out in the open then, right in the middle of the street and heading for the yard toward our house, and I heard these other horsemen coming

The March to Montgomery

> and I knew they were going to catch me. I just knew they were going to either trample me or hit me with a club or whip. My legs didn't seem to be moving — it was like in a bad dream when you are chased by something and can't run. Well, just as I got to the yard this white [SNCC worker] named Frank Soracco came by me and he was moving fast. And I must have been crying out, because he stopped and just swept me up and carried me under the armpits and kept moving. — Rachel West. [9]

Some Blacks begin to retaliate with thrown rocks and bottles, but Movement leaders and civil rights workers move among them, urging nonviolent discipline. The cops are raging with mob fury, all control abandoned to racist hate. Many are now carrying loaded rifles and shotguns at the ready. The activists know that if a single white officer is injured by a tossed brick there'll be a blood-bath of indiscriminate gunfire.

Eventually, the frenzy of cop violence subsides and the forces of "law and order" occupy the Carver Project and Selma's Black commercial district, forcing all Blacks inside and off the street. They allow the MCHR ambulances to ferry the most seriously wounded — more than 90 — to Good Samaritan Hospital and Burwell Infirmary (a Black old-age home).

Among those hospitalized is John Lewis with a skull fracture and concussion. Before he allows himself to be taken to hospital, he tells the battered and bruised people gathered in Brown Chapel, *"I don't know how President Johnson can send troops to Vietnam. I don't see how he can send troops to the Congo. I don't see how he can send troops to Africa, and he can't send troops to Selma, Alabama. Next time we march, we may have to keep going when we get to Montgomery. We have to go to Washington."* His words are reported in *The* New York Times and the Johnson administration responds by announcing that they will send FBI agents to Selma to, *"... investigate whether unnecessary force was used by law officers and others."*

The Selma Voting Rights Struggle

As the afternoon wanes and evening falls, Brown Chapel remains crowded with marchers and supporters huddling together for mutual support. Acrid tear gas fumes still emanate from clothes and skin. Eyes weep and breathing is labored. There is anger and rage, of course, but also deep humiliation at being whipped, beaten, and driven like slaves. Outside, the troopers and deputies strut like conquering heroes. Inside, people are dispirited, dejected, filled with despair. They have endured so much — violence, jail, economic retaliation and yet despite all of this, no one has been registered to vote and no one outside Selma seems to care.

Sheyann Webb recalls:

> I sat with Rachel up toward the front. ... we were just sitting there crying, listening to the others cry; some were even moaning and wailing. It was an awful thing. It was like we were at our own funeral. But then later in the night, maybe nine-thirty or ten, I don't know for sure, all of a sudden somebody there started humming. I think they were moaning and it just went into the humming of a freedom song. It was real low, but some of us children began humming along, slow and soft. At first I didn't even know what it was, what song, I mean. It was like a funeral sound, a dirge. Then I recognized it — "Ain't Gonna Let Nobody Turn Me' Round." I'd never heard it or hummed it that way before. But it just started to catch on, and the people began to pick it up. It started to swell, the humming.

> Then we began singing the words. We sang, "Ain't gonna let George Wallace turn me 'round." And, "Ain't gonna let Jim Clark turn me 'round. Ain't gonna let no state trooper turn me 'round. Ain't gonna let no horses. ... ain't gonna let no tear gas — ain't gonna let nobody turn me 'round." Nobody!

> And everybody's singing now, and some of them are

clapping their hands, and they're still crying, but it's a different kind of crying. It's the kind of crying that's got spirit, not the weeping they had been doing. And me and Rachel are crying and singing and it just gets louder and louder. I know the state troopers outside the church heard it. Everybody heard it. Because more people were coming in then, leaving their apartments and coming to the church — because something was happening.

We was singing and telling the world that we hadn't been whipped ... I think we all realized it at the same time, that we had won something that day, because people were standing up and singing like I'd never heard them before. ... When I first went into that church that evening those people sitting there were beaten — I mean their spirit, their will was beaten. But when that singing started, we grew stronger. Each one of us said to ourselves that we could go back out there and face the tear gas, face the horses, face whatever Jim Clark could throw at us. — Sheyann Webb. [9]

Call...

SELMA: Unknown to the battered freedom fighters gathered in Brown Chapel, there is a political *tsunami* racing outward from Selma, Alabama. Print and radio reporters jam the lines as they file their stories by phone. TV crews evade the trooper's highway blockade and rush their film to Montgomery where chartered planes fly it to New York for processing.

In the mid-1960s, there was no live or immediately-thereafter broadcast of images from breaking news events. Camera crews recorded events on film rather than magnetic videotape or digital device, and the film was sent to a TV studio or laboratory for processing before it could be broadcast. For national news, that required flying the film by courier to New York or Los Angeles. So the first visuals of Bloody Sunday did not hit the airwaves until evening Eastern time.

The Selma Voting Rights Struggle

ATLANTA: Throughout the late afternoon, urgent phone conversations are held between Movement leaders in Selma and Dr. King and his executive staff in Atlanta. After more than 4,000 arrests, the brutal attack in Marion, the police murder of Jimmy Lee Jackson, and now a massive assault stretching from the Edmund Pettus bridge into the heart of Selma's Black community, there can be no doubt that Governor Wallace and Sheriff Clark are determined to suppress the voting rights movement with savage police violence. That cannot be allowed.

Dr. King decides. They have to defy Wallace and Clark by marching again. But not alone. For the first time ever, he mobilizes all of SCLC's resources to issue a nationwide call for people of conscience to stand with local Blacks as they nonviolently confront troopers, deputies, and possemen. In previous years, small groups of northerners had been asked to support protests in places like Birmingham and St. Augustine, but never before has King made a general plea for thousands of people to place their bodies on the line against police violence. As night falls, hundreds of telegrams are being dispatched from Atlanta, reading in part:

The people of Selma will struggle on for the soul of the nation, but it is fitting that all Americans help to bear the burden. I call therefore, on clergy of all faiths, representatives of every part of the country, to join me in Selma for a ministers' march to Montgomery on Tuesday morning, March ninth.

Randolph Blackwell of SCLC in Atlanta recalls:

> I had the stay-at-home job. I kept the store. ... if you got two thousand trade unions and you can afford from a budget standpoint to send two hundred telegrams, it then becomes a question of which two hundred unions do you wire and say, "Come." If you've got five hundred women's organizations and you can afford to send twenty-five telegrams, which twenty-five out of five hundred do you wire and say, "Come." And that's a matter

The March to Montgomery

> of making the distinction between which organizations have a history of protest and which organizations have no history. No need of sending a telegram to the Railroad Machinists. They've never marched in their own defense, so they certainly aren't going to come to Selma to march with you on your issues. You don't send a telegram to the League of Women Voters, 'cause marching ain't their thing, but you send it to the Women's Strike For Peace, 'cause they've been out in the street for the past fifty years. You raise the issue, they'll raise their banner... — Randolph Blackwell, SCLC. [15]

Tuesday, March 9 is chosen to give northern supporters time to reach Selma, and also time for SCLC attorneys to file a motion in federal court on Monday morning to prevent the state of Alabama from blocking the march. Unlike the Dallas County voter-registration cases, which had to be filed in the federal district court of Judge Thomas in Mobile, this motion will go before Federal Judge Frank Johnson in the Middle District of Alabama in Montgomery. Judge Johnson is considered a "southern liberal." SCLC leaders are confident he will grant their motion to allow a march from Selma to Montgomery. In the past, Johnson has ruled against bus segregation during both the Montgomery Bus Boycott and the Freedom Rides, and he has supported Black voting rights in a number of cases. He has no love for Wallace — who once referred to him as a *"carpetbagging, scalawagging, integrating, liar"* — and even less for the violent racists who bombed his mother's home in the mistaken belief that he lived there. U.S. Marshals now guard his actual home around the clock.

When word of the brutal attack arrives from Selma, members of the SNCC Executive Committee are meeting in Atlanta.

> Naturally Bloody Sunday rendered, at least for a New York minute, all doctrinal and strategic differences moot. For many in SNCC it was *deja vu* all over again,

The Selma Voting Rights Struggle

> the Freedom Rides revisited, the "violence-cannot-be-allowed-to-stop-the-movement" reflex. — Kwame Ture (Stokely Carmichael). [1]

Bypassing SNCC's normal consensus-style decision-making process, Jim Forman issues a mobilization call for all SNCC members to converge on Selma, resume the march, and confront the cops and troopers. He charters a plane to fly himself and other SNCC leaders from Atlanta to Selma.

SNCC veteran and Selma organizer Prathia Hall recalls:

> On Bloody Sunday, March 7, 1965, I was at the Atlanta SNCC office when a call came from ... Selma. Over the phone we could hear screams of people who were being attacked. SNCC immediately chartered a plane so that people could go to Selma right away. As the group was ready to leave, Judy Richardson said, "Wait a minute, there are no women in this group. Where's Prathia?" And so I went.
>
> It was a very traumatic time for me. When we got there we saw what had happened. It was a bloody mess; people's heads had been beaten; they'd been gassed. Of course we held a rally. At the meeting people were angry; they, too, had been traumatized. One man stood up and said, "I was out on the bridge today because I thought it was right. But while I was on the bridge, Jim Clark came to my house and tear-gassed my eighty-year-old mother, and next time he comes to my house, I'm going to be ready." Everybody understood what that meant. People had lived their lives basically sleeping with guns beside their beds — that was just a part of the culture. These were people who were struggling to be nonviolent, who in their hearts and spirits were not a violent people, but they also had notions of self-defense. — Prathia Hall. [17]

The March to Montgomery

JACKSON: SNCC's large Mississippi staff is holding a statewide meeting in Jackson when word of Selma — and Forman's call to mobilize — reaches them. By evening, carloads of SNCC veterans are rushing east on Highway 80 at dangerously high speeds.

TUSKEGEE: Tuskegee Institute is the premier Black college in Alabama, and its 2,300 students are just a 90-minute drive from Selma. Back in February, when the Voting Rights Campaign began to heat up, students organized the Tuskegee Institute Advancement League (TIAL) to engage local issues and support the struggle for voting rights in the Black Belt. TIAL members attended mass meetings in Selma and participated in protests there. When the March to Montgomery was first announced, TIAL began mobilizing students, faculty, and the Tuskegee community to join the Selma marchers upon their arrival in Montgomery. After Bloody Sunday, those efforts intensify.

> Everybody had seen what happened on television, and there was a lot of talk about the beatings on that bridge. Tuskegee students felt that they should react somehow. King had called for people from all over the state to go to Montgomery and have a massive demonstration. So TIAL tried to mobilize students. We assigned two TIAL people to each dorm and went around to all the dormitories that Sunday night, talking about the need to get involved. We had a whole series of meetings. Just about all the people in the dorms turned out. — Tuskegee student leader George Ware. [19]

NATION: Across the country, Freedom Movement activists respond. Some begin mobilizing support demonstrations at federal buildings in their home communities. Others head for Alabama. Linda Dehnad, of the New York SNCC office, recalls:

> I was on the [Friends of SNCC] steering committee in New York. I worked with students. My house on Riverside Drive and 90th Street [was] the place [for SNCC folk] to stay when they were in New York. So my house

always had SNCC people in it. On Bloody Sunday my dining room was filled with people. We were watching TV. We just turned on the news. So we're watching the news and somebody said, "Oh my God. That's John." Within 10 minutes, my house was empty. They grabbed their stuff and they went. — Linda Dehnad. [3]

The Sunday night movie on ABC is the network premiere of *Judgment at Nuremburg,* a major TV event with an estimated audience of 48 million. Correspondent Frank Reynolds interrupts the program with news from Selma followed by 15 minutes of Bloody Sunday film. Some viewers are at first confused, assuming the images are of Nazi atrocities. CBS and NBC also provide dramatic coverage — as do the Monday morning newspapers.

For many Americans who have never before marched, never before protested, Bloody Sunday is the tipping point that moves them into action: Not Bloody Sunday alone, of course, but the cumulative effect of all that has gone before. Students, clergy, housewives, and men and women from all walks of life, both Black and white, determine to take a stand. Some hear of and respond to King's call; others act spontaneously. Some hit the road for Selma, some protest locally, some demand immediate action from their U.S. senators and representatives.

Monday, March 8

VIETNAM: Across the international dateline, Sunday afternoon March 7 in Alabama is Monday morning, March 8, in Southeast Asia. Halfway around the world from Bloody Sunday in Selma, U.S. Marines in full combat gear wade ashore on Da Nang beach. They are the first of what will eventually rise to more than 500,000 American combat troops fighting to "defend democracy" in Vietnam. Over the course of the next 10 years, more than 2.5 million members of the U.S. armed forces serve in this undeclared war.

The March to Montgomery

Behind the scenes, President Johnson pressures Dr. King to cancel the Tuesday march. Just a few months earlier, LBJ had campaigned on repeated promises never to send American boys to fight in Indochina — though as the Pentagon Papers later reveal he had already decided to do just that. Now the first U.S. combat troops are landing in Vietnam. The administration has prepared a carefully planned media campaign to justify his action both domestically and internationally. TV cameras are stationed on Da Nang beach to capture the dramatic scene while pro-American Vietnamese greet them at the tide-line with "Welcome U.S. Marines" banners. But now on this Monday throughout the world, news stories and images of Marines wading ashore to "defend democracy" in Vietnam clash with images of real-life American democracy in action on the Edmund Pettus bridge in Selma, Alabama. Johnson is furious, and he wants no risk of any repeat violence on Tuesday that might compete with his public relations strategy, or continue to give the lie to his "freedom" rhetoric.

WASHINGTON: By Monday morning, pickets are marching in front of the Justice Department. Three SNCC members manage to enter Attorney General Katzenbach's office and stage a sit-in. As the cops drag them out, SNCC worker Frank Smith shouts: *"It did not take the Attorney General long to get his policemen up here to throw us out. Why can't he give us the same protection in Alabama?"* Twenty more SNCC activists enter the building and occupy the 5th floor corridor outside the AG's office until they are eventually dragged out around 9 pm. Pickets from SNCC, CORE, SCLC, NAACP and other organizations appear outside other DC buildings. Protesters demanding federal intervention to protect Black voting rights block traffic by lying down on Pennsylvania Avenue outside the White House.

Under pressure from the White House and members of Congress, whose constituents demand action, Katzenbach huddles with Justice Department lawyers. They now accept that something has to be done about Black voting rights this year — not at some vague future date. But what?

Back in February, as political pressure from the Selma campaign started to be felt in Washington, a reluctant Justice Department began mulling over the idea of a new constitutional amendment, perhaps something like the 19th Amendment granting woman suffrage.

But civil rights activists adamantly oppose that idea as a stalling tactic. The Constitution *already* guarantees full citizenship to non-whites; the problem is enforcing those promises. A new national voting law is needed, one that will enable *and require* the federal government to protect the voting rights of racial minorities. Both a bill and an amendment first have to be fought through Congress and both have to overcome a southern filibuster. But a bill immediately becomes law while an amendment must then be ratified by three quarters of the states, a process that may well take years and could easily fail. And, if an amendment is eventually ratified, Congress will then have to endure and overcome yet another filibuster to enact the legislation to implement it.

NATION: Protests, sit-ins, and marches demanding justice for Blacks in Alabama swell and expand and continue for days at federal buildings and U.S. courthouses in New York, Chicago, Los Angeles, San Francisco, Boston, Philadelphia, and dozens of other cities.

MONTGOMERY: Lawyers working with SCLC file *Hosea Williams v George Wallace* before U.S. District Judge Johnson in Montgomery, petitioning him to prevent Alabama cops from blocking a renewed march on Tuesday, March 9. They are stunned when he refuses to rule on their plea without first holding a formal hearing on the issue. Instead of allowing a march the following day, he asks that it be held off. Without a federal injunction, Wallace and his troopers are free to block the Tuesday effort by any means they choose.

The March to Montgomery

SELMA: Dr. King is now in Selma, and by phone from Washington, Attorney General Katzenbach browbeats him hour after hour to call off the Tuesday march. DOJ official John Doar and Community Relations Service head Leroy Collins bring personal pressure to bear. They promise administration support for a new voting rights bill, but imply that might be conditional on there being no second march.

The Community Relations Service was created by the Civil Rights Act of 1964 "to provide assistance to communities in resolving disputes, disagreements, or difficulties relating to discriminatory practices based on race, color, or national origin which impair the rights of persons in such communities under the Constitution or laws of the United States."

... and Response

WASHINGTON: Moving with what for them is astounding speed, the National Council of Churches' Commission on Religion and Race responds to King's appeal by immediately issuing a press statement endorsing his call. They dispatch a flood of telegrams to Protestant congregations nationwide urging clergy and laity to march with Dr. King in Selma. A plane chartered by the DC Council of Churches takes wing for Alabama carrying 40 ministers, rabbis, and priests. Among them are Methodist Bishop John Wesley Lord, Rabbi Richard Hirsch and Msgr. George Gingras. For years, most members of the Roman Catholic hierarchy have tried to restrict priests and nuns from participating in civil rights protests. But now, facing imminent ecclesiastic rebellion, Washington Archbishop Patrick O'Boyle reluctantly grants an exception, *"just this once,"* allowing Catholic clergy to participate in Tuesday's march. When he learns what O'Boyle has done, the Bishop of Alabama refuses his consent. But, it's too late, priests and nuns are on their way and they refuse to turn back now.

NATION: Rabbi Israel Dresner, a veteran of protest and jail in Albany GA, the Freedom Rides, and St. Augustine, joins a Black

The Selma Voting Rights Struggle

AME Zion minister on a flight to Atlanta where they rent a car and drive through the night to Selma. Famed theologian Robert McAffee Brown suspends his classes at Stanford and heads for the airport, as do hundreds of others, far and wide, including Metz Rollins and Robert Stone, who less than a year earlier, had been in Mississippi coordinating the "perpetual picket" in Hattiesburg. From Chicago Theologic Seminary, CORE veteran and now divinity student Jesse Jackson leads a car caravan of students and teachers on a 750-mile drive across Indiana, Kentucky, Tennessee, and down through the heart of Alabama to Selma. From Boston, more than 100 Unitarians and other clergy book flights to Montgomery. Among them are Rev. James Reeb and Episcopal seminary student Jonathan Daniels.

SELMA: On this Monday in March, 150 carloads of state troopers and a swarm of possemen occupy Selma like an army. Local students and SNCC activists — many just arrived from Atlanta and Mississippi — lead impromptu freedom marches through the Carver Housing Project. Made up mostly of young people, they try to maneuver through the cops blocking their way to downtown. Caravans of cop cars loaded with club-wielding troopers race with lights flashing and sirens screaming along the dirt streets of the Black community, blocking every nonviolent effort to reach the courthouse and the commercial district.

Meanwhile, a day-long mass meeting in Brown Chapel starts early Monday and runs late into the night as people re-live the violence, come to terms with beatings and humiliation, and renew their determination to be free. SCLC and local leaders preach the power of nonviolence as the only effective answer to police savagery.

> Any man who has the urge to hit a posseman or a state trooper with a pop bottle is a fool. That is just what they want you to do. Then they can call you a mob and beat you to death. — Rev. James Bevel. [8]

By mid-morning, carloads of outside supporters — most of them white — begin unloading in front of the church steps where

The March to Montgomery

yesterday mounted possemen had lashed men and women with whips and rifle-toting troopers had threatened even children with death.

> They had seen the news and left home before the broadcast officially ended for the evening. I saw new life leap into the faces of the people and they were ready to sacrifice more. During the next 48 hours, hundreds and hundreds of people from heaven knows how many different states in the Union came to Selma. Black families opened their homes and gave their beds to people who had come to Selma. ... Local residents opened their homes and travelers from afar accepted the warm embrace and kindness that was extended. The only phrase a newcomer to Selma had to utter was, "I am here to march." That phrase secured the speaker a home, a bed, and food with no questions asked. — Rev. F.D. Reese, DCVL. [22]

As the mass meeting continues into the afternoon, whites — bishops, ministers, rabbis, wives of U.S. Senators, union leaders, and students from famous universities — now mingle with Blacks in the main floor pews and the balcony benches. Each new group is introduced to speak a few words of support from the pulpit. Bishop John Wesley Lord proclaims, *"You can say that I heard the Macedonian call. We heard the call of God from Selma and we came."* They are met with wild applause and thunderous singing.

Third-grade student Sheyann Webb recalled:

> The next day, Monday, March eighth, people from all over the country — mostly ministers and some nuns — began arriving to help us. They were all over the apartment yards and at the church and we were asked — those who lived there — to provide room for them. I remember that very few of the children went to school that morning. They were running back and forth between Brown Chapel and their homes, helping the newcomers

with their baggage and finding places for them to stay.
— Sheyann Webb. [9]

At 10:30 pm, the mass meeting in Brown Chapel is still packed to overflowing with Alabama Blacks and hundreds of northern supporters who are still arriving in Selma. Taking a line from Langston Hughes, Dr. King defies Wallace and rebuffs President Johnson's demand that the march be canceled:

> Life for me ain't been no crystal stair. ... If a man is 36 years old, as I happen to be, and some great truth stands before the door of his life ... and he refuses to stand up because he wants to live a little longer and he's afraid that his home will get bombed or he's afraid that he will lose his job, he's afraid that he will get shot or beaten down by state troopers, he may go on and live until he's 80, but he's just as dead at 36 as he would be at 80. And the state of breathing in his life is merely the announcement of an earlier death of the spirit. — Martin Luther King, Jr. [8]

Tuesday, March 9

WASHINGTON: By Tuesday morning, the 20 SNCC activists expelled from the building on Monday night for sitting-in outside Katzenbach's office have now returned 200 strong to fill the corridor. More than 700 men, women, and children are now picketing the White House.

In the Oval Office, Johnson's attention is divided. He is determined to prevent any repetition of Sunday's embarrassing violence in Selma. Through his surrogates, he continues to demand that Dr. King cancel the march. But his main focus is the war he is greatly expanding in Vietnam. As previously planned, this day and the next is given to personally briefing every single member of Congress in groups of 50 each. Along with Secretary of State Dean Rusk and Secretary of Defense Robert McNamara, he assures the senators and representatives, *"The most important*

The March to Montgomery

thing I can say to you about South Vietnam is that there are no tricks in it, nothing up our sleeves, no essential facts being concealed." [8]

When the Pentagon Papers are stolen and published in 1971, they reveal that the administration's statements on Vietnam were a fabric of lies, distortions, and deceit — as McNamara eventually admits many decades later.

NATION: Hundreds rally at the FBI office in Manhattan, blocking traffic on 69th Street and 3rd Avenue. More than 10,000 march through downtown Detroit, with Michigan Governor George Romney placing himself at the head of the line. In Chicago, protesters snarl the Loop by sitting-down in the intersection of State and Madison. Protests demanding federal action to protect voting rights erupt in Boston, Cleveland, Detroit, Los Angeles, New Haven, San Francisco, Syracuse, and elsewhere across the nation.

Judge Johnson's Injunction

MONTGOMERY: Court convenes on Tuesday morning to hear SCLC's plea that the march to Montgomery be allowed to proceed without interference by the state of Alabama. SCLC's attorneys are stunned when Judge Johnson issues an injunction *against* the Freedom Movement. He blocks the march until after he holds formal hearings on their *Williams v Wallace* petition. In a rare instance of independent judicial activism, he issues his order without any request or plea from any party to the case. The order is unconstitutional on its face because it denies the marchers their First Amendment rights without just cause. As a legal scholar, he knows it will be overturned on appeal, but that will take days or weeks and the march is scheduled to commence in hours.

Everyone knows that the FBI taps Movement phones. King's conversations and plans — including his determination to defy Washington pressure and march on Tuesday — are reported

The Selma Voting Rights Struggle

directly to White House and DOJ officials. Many activists suspect that Judge Johnson's blatantly political ruling is issued in collusion with the President as a way of *forcing* King to abandon the march.

SELMA: Judge Johnson's injunction creates a lose-lose dilemma for Movement leaders in Selma. Activists and organizers all agree that an immediate return march — larger than the first one — is the only way to counter police brutality. If violence is allowed to stand unchallenged, it will halt organizing momentum throughout the Black Belt, and if Alabama can successfully use state terror to intimidate the Movement, so will other states. With national support now behind them, Alabama Blacks demand a new march to defy Wallace and erase the degrading humiliation of Bloody Sunday's clubs, gas, whips and horses. They *need* to march, they need to *prove* to white racists — and themselves — that they, *"ain't gonna let nobody turn me 'round."* If the march is canceled, movement leaders fear morale and momentum will plummet.

Almost a thousand northerners, many of them important religious leaders, have come to Selma to put their bodies on the line alongside Alabama Blacks. They are frightened and scared but they are also determined. They have summoned their courage to face their starkest fears of violent danger and criminal arrest. Their emotions are at a fever pitch — they are ready to march! March now! If the march is postponed for a week or two while Judge Johnson deliberates, will they return to Selma when the march is permitted? No one knows.

But the whole point of the Selma campaign is to win voting rights — not to march to Montgomery. More than 4,000 people have gone to jail to win the right to vote; Jimmy Lee Jackson was killed fighting for the vote; 600 men, women, and children endured Bloody Sunday for the vote. The march to Montgomery is not the goal; it's just a tactic to achieve the greater purpose.

Through spokesmen, President Johnson sends a promise from Washington that he will support new, strong, voting-

The March to Montgomery

rights legislation. But his surrogates also warn King that if he marches on Tuesday, LBJ may weaken — or possibly oppose — a new voting rights bill. Even with the President behind it, a voting bill has to overcome a southern filibuster to pass in the Senate. That filibuster cannot be broken without the votes of Republican senators. Republicans, and particularly their leader Everett Dirksen, are strong for "law and order." They are already uncomfortable with Blacks disobeying local segregation ordinances and police commands; they might well view breaking a federal injunction as defiance of their own national authority (and so too might some northern Democrats). Even if Tuesday's march wins through to Montgomery — which no one believes is possible — doing so at the cost of eventual defeat in the Senate is a disaster, not a victory. And, despite Judge Johnson's political stab in the back, confidence remains high that he will *eventually* rule in favor of the Freedom Movement's right to march to Montgomery.

Moreover, if a voting rights law does pass, it will be up to the federal courts to order enforcement. Federal judges are fiercely jealous of their authority; they don't take kindly to defiance of any kind, and they have long memories. Their rulings and interpretations will put teeth in the law — or not. Dr. King has never violated a federal court order. His overarching strategy is to use the power of federal laws and courts to force the South to change. For years, segregationist politicians have mobilized white resistance to the Supreme Court and the federal judiciary. They've called for "interposition" and "nullification" and "standing in the schoolhouse door." If Dr. King and the Freedom Movement now disobey a federal injunction, might not the federal judges equate them with James Eastland, Robert Byrd, and George Wallace?

Movement leaders meet in the Selma home of Dr. Sullivan Jackson. Tension is high; debate is hot. James Forman of SNCC demands an immediate all-out march come hell or high water. James Farmer of CORE counsels caution and patience — any attempt to break through the wall of troopers will be a bloody failure for no gain and maybe great political loss.

The Selma Voting Rights Struggle

The unrelenting pressure from Washington continues unabated. On the phone, Katzenbach urges King to obey the injunction. He cannot understand why they simply cannot wait a few more days on the promise of eventual relief. King replies, *"But Mr. Attorney General, you have not been a Black man in America for 300 years."* CRS chief Collins personally delivers a message from LBJ that the Bloody Sunday violence disgraced the United States in the eyes of the world. The President's overriding concern is to prevent more violence; he wants the marchers to stay home to guarantee the peace. Rev. Shuttlesworth shouts back, *"You're talking to the wrong people! Take it up with Wallace and Clark. They're the ones in the disgrace business!"*

Everyone weighs in, but the weight is on Dr. King. As he decides, so it will be. He tells Doar and Collins that he has to keep faith with the people of Selma. He has to march. Collins immediately offers a compromise. Judge Johnson's order does not prohibit marching within Selma. So King can march over the bridge to the Selma city line at the far bank of the Alabama River and then turn around and return to the church when ordered to do so in conformance with the injunction. He assures King that the troopers and Clark's posse of ragtag racists won't attack.

"I don't believe you can get those people not to charge into us even if we do stop," King tells him. He knows that Clark and Lingo may whip heads regardless of what promise they make to Collins. He also fears that even if he disappoints the marchers and loses precious momentum by turning around, Judge Johnson will consider him in violation for crossing the bridge, and President Johnson will turn on him for failure to meekly accept the "no march" command. Either way he's caught. Reluctantly, he agrees to Collins' plan.

Turnaround Tuesday

SELMA: Jam-packed mass meetings simultaneously get under way in Brown Chapel and nearby First Baptist. The participants are mostly Black, men and women who have defied

The March to Montgomery

physical and economic terror for the vote. Young students, who have cut class to march and go to jail, rock the sanctuaries with their singing. Hundreds of men, women, young and old, have come in from the surrounding Black Belt counties, from Perry and Wilcox, from Marengo, Sumter, Hale and Green, and also from Birmingham, Tuskegee, Tuscaloosa, Montgomery, Mobile, and elsewhere in Alabama. Carloads of Black marchers are arriving from Freedom Movement centers in Mississippi, Georgia, Florida, Louisiana, and the Carolinas.

SNCC organizer Maria Varela recalls:

> On the morning of the second march, as I stood at the door of Brown Chapel I was struck by the fact that coming up the steps were mostly middle-aged and elderly black men and women. Listening to them, it became apparent that they were angry and ashamed that the children had taken the beatings for protesting the denial of the vote to adults. I remember one woman in particular. No bigger than five feet tall, she appeared to be in her seventies. She wore a black overcoat with flimsy 'going to town' shoes and brought a thin cotton bedroll tied up with her toothbrush and umbrella. That was all she brought for a march that, if we made it across the bridge, would go on for days. I don't remember ever seeing her before at any of the mass meetings in Selma. My guess was that this was her first time coming out for anything. She came for the children. And she seemed to really believe that she was going to survive that wall of mounted police and walk the fifty miles to Montgomery.
> — Maria Varela. [17]

Buses and cars continue to arrive, unloading weary northerners — most of them white — who have pressed on through the night to reach Selma in time for the march. Vans and taxis shuttle back and forth along US 80 bringing marchers from the Montgomery airport. Clark's deputies tail and harass cars with northern plates; drivers coming in from Montgomery have to maneuver around the small army of state troopers waiting on the far side of the bridge.

Anticipating casualties, Medical Committee for Human Rights (MCHR) doctors and nurses set up a large, emergency-aid station in the basement of First Baptist. For weeks to come, they staff and maintain this center, dealing not just with Movement-related medical problems but all the hidden health issues of racism, poverty, and exploitation that Alabama's segregated system conceals and denies.

> Early one morning I was [at the aid station] and a young Black woman came in, real hesitant, furtively — scared. She was carrying a sick infant, maybe a week or so old, and bad sick. It turned out she was a sharecropper or tenant living on a rural plantation out in the county somewhere. Her newborn baby was dying, but the landowner refused to let her leave the plantation. Either because he didn't want to pay any medical expenses for her, or he didn't want her to become contaminated with Freedom Movement ideas. Or both. Somehow she heard about the MCHR doctors at First Baptist through the grapevine — the secret rumor line that ran like an invisible network beneath the notice of the white power structure. In the dead of night, like a runaway slave, she snuck away carrying her child all the way to Selma on foot. She was terrified of what the owner would do to her when he found out she had escaped. The nurse had to keep reassuring her that she wouldn't be sent back. My assignment was elsewhere, and I had to leave without knowing what happened to her or her child. — Bruce Hartford, SCLC. [4]

It's mid-afternoon as more than 3,000 marchers begin assembling on the playground next to Brown Chapel. MCHR medics with canvas satchels for first-aid are spaced along the line. Roughly two-thirds of the marchers are Black, the rest are white with a few Latinos and Asians. Dr. King addresses them:

The March to Montgomery

> Almighty God, thou has called us to walk for freedom, even as thou did the children of Israel. ... We have the right to walk the highways, and we have the right to walk to Montgomery if our feet will get us there. I have no alternative but to lead a march from this spot to carry our grievances to the seat of government. I have made my choice. I have got to march. I do not know what lies ahead of us. There may be beatings, jails, tear gas. But I say to you this afternoon that I would rather die on the highways of Alabama than make a butchery of my conscience. ... If you can't be nonviolent, don't get in here. If you can't accept blows without retaliating, don't get in the line. — Martin Luther King. [8] [10]

Dr. King then articulates the justice and purpose of marching to Montgomery, but he fails to inform the marchers of his agreement to turn the march around when ordered to halt — an omission that will lead to confusion, contention, and bitterness. And, one that greatly increases distrust between SNCC and SCLC.

Singing "Ain't Gonna Let Nobody Turn Me 'Round," they march four-abreast through the streets of Selma heading toward the bridge. Dr. King leads the line with prominent ministers, priests, rabbis, and nuns. At the foot of the bridge, a federal marshal halts them and reads to King the full text of Judge Johnson's injunction. *"I am aware of the order,"* King replies. He strides forward up the rise.

When they reach the bridge crest they see ahead of them, more than 500 state troopers — practically the entire Alabama force — lined up across the highway behind barricades. Lurking nearby are Sheriff's deputies and a mob of possemen. King leads the long line down toward the waiting phalanx. Major John Cloud of the troopers orders the protesters to halt. King argues their right to march, but Cloud refuses. The marchers stretch back for almost a mile up and over the bridge, into town, and down Water Street. Starting at the front and moving backward down the line, they kneel for prayers offered by Rev. Abernathy, Bishop Lord, Dr. Docherty, and Rabbi Hirsch.

The Selma Voting Rights Struggle

Singing "We Shall Overcome," the protesters then rise. Suddenly, Major Cloud shouts, *"Troopers, withdraw!"* In what is clearly a pre-planned maneuver, the cops quickly pull back the portable barricades blocking the highway and seemingly open the way to Montgomery — though their menacing ranks line the road on either side. King has just a split second to decide. Sensing a trap to lure him into clearly violating the injunction and thereby justifying a violent police attack, he shouts, *"We'll go back to the church now!"* He leads the marchers in a U-turn back up and over the bridge.

As the marching lines pass each other — one returning to Brown Chapel, the other moving forward toward the turnaround spot — those whose view had been blocked by the bridge-rise call out to those returning, asking what had happened? No one knows, but everyone maintains the self-discipline of nonviolent action. For this march, Dr. King is the captain, and no one breaks ranks to dispute his decision — that is for later, off the street.

For most of the marchers, the feeling is one of overwhelming relief that the police have not attacked. But, for many there is also a deep sense of betrayal; they had keyed themselves up to the highest peak of their courage and now they are being ordered to meekly retreat. Among SNCC members, now including a good portion of the Mississippi staff, feelings range from disgust to fury:

> When we walked over that bridge on that day we were getting ready to go, everybody was getting ready for the fight. We were waiting for the shit to get on. We were ready for the rumble. Somebody walks up to King, they kneel down at the front of the march on the down-slope of the bridge. They kneel down and somebody must have whispered in Martin Luther King's ear and they turned around and said we're going to go back to the church. ... The [people were saying], "Let's go, let's go," and [the leadership] were saying, "No." And then we heard that we weren't going [to continue toward Montgomery]. ...

The March to Montgomery

> We were mad, we were all ready to get our ass kicked that afternoon. And we marched back to Brown Chapel. It was not only SNCC people. There were ministers, some Catholic priests, they were mad because they thought they were going to be martyrs for the cause that morning. — Hardy Frye, SNCC. [16]

Back at Brown Chapel, where latecomers from the North are still arriving, King tells the mass meeting that the march was *"The greatest demonstration for freedom, the greatest confrontation so far in the South."* Not everyone sees it so. From the audience come questions, challenges, and disagreements. One young man asks, *"Why didn't we just sit down on the highway and wait until the injunction was lifted?"*

King does not answer directly, replying instead that they will eventually reach Montgomery. He asks those northern supporters who are able to do so to remain in Selma until the march can take place.

When James Forman of SNCC speaks, he addresses a deeper issue than the tactics of turning around, or not:

> I've paid my dues in Selma. I've been to jail here. I've been beaten here, so I have the right to ask this: why was there violence on Sunday and none on Tuesday? You know the answer. They don't beat white people. It's Negroes they beat and kill. [8]

A Black citizen of Selma responds:

> You're right, they didn't beat us today because the world was here with us. But that's what we want. Don't let these white people feel that we don't appreciate their coming. [8]

The Selma Voting Rights Struggle

Savage Assault on Unitarian Ministers

SELMA: As evening falls in Selma, there is much confusion, coming, and going among the northerners who answered Dr. King's call. Most of them had assumed they would march that day in solidarity and then be in jail or immediately return home to their normal lives. Now they are being asked to remain indefinitely until Judge Johnson's anti-march injunction is lifted. For many, particularly the major religious leaders, it is impossible to stay over and they regretfully depart to resume their ecclesiastic responsibilities. But, knowing that their presence provides at least some limited deterrence to police violence, others decide to sojourn in Selma at least for a night or two.

Among those who change their plans and remain in Selma are Unitarian ministers James Reeb and Orloff Miller of Boston and Clark Olsen of Berkeley. After dinner at the crowded, Black-owned Walkers Cafe, they stroll back toward the Movement offices at Alabama and Franklin streets. They pass by the Silver Moon Cafe, a hangout for Klan and possemen. Selma Blacks know not to walk that block after dark. When Movement activists arrive from out of town, the local families they stay with warn them of such danger spots. But, in the confusion of the day, with hundreds of northerners arriving in a short time and abrupt changes in travel plans, the three white ministers are unaware of the danger.

Four men with baseball bats and makeshift clubs step from the shadows and advance on the three ministers. *"Hey you niggers!"* They strike Olsen and Miller and bludgeon Reeb in the head. As they run off, one of them shouts, *"Now you know what it's like to be a real nigger!"*

The publicly funded hospital in segregated, "separate-but-equal" Selma provides only limited service to Blacks. Known as the "white" hospital, it's unwilling to treat civil rights "agitators" at all — regardless of race. Outside the major cities, ambulance service is rarely available to Alabama Blacks, so the hearses of Black-owned funeral parlors are often used for emergency medical transport. But they are not equipped with medical equipment, supplies, or trained medics.

Miller and Olsen are bleeding but not seriously injured. Reeb is dazed and confused and can barely see. They make it to the SCLC office where Diane Nash quickly sends Reeb to the Burwell Infirmary in a hearse from the downstairs funeral parlor. The Black doctor at Burwell determines that Reeb needs immediate neurosurgery. The nearest emergency unit willing to undertake an operation of that kind is in Birmingham 90 miles away. They refuse to treat him without an advance cash payment of $150 (equal to a bit over $1,000 in 2012.) The ministers don't have anywhere near that amount and neither credit cards nor medical insurance are available in the mid-1960s. By now Reeb has fallen unconscious.

Somehow, Diane manages to scrounge up the fee and the hearse rushes Reeb, Olsen, and Miller north toward Birmingham. Not far out of town, one of its old tires blows out. In a dangerous area of rural Alabama for an integrated group to be stranded at night, they run on the rim until they reach a Black radio station where they can summon a new hearse-ambulance. Dallas County sheriff's deputies spot them and interrogate the Black driver and the white ministers, but refuse to provide an escort or protection. Cars driven by hostile whites begin to cruise back and forth past the parking lot where they wait.

It takes almost two hours to locate a replacement ambulance, find a driver with the courage to make the run, and get it to Birmingham. The unconscious Reeb hovers near death. Olsen and Miller have to brace the stretcher to keep it from rolling around as they head north at high speed on the narrow county road. They have no trained medic, and the two ministers don't know how to prevent infection from entering Reeb's lungs. They arrive at University Hospital in Birmingham past 11 pm, four hours after the attack. Reeb has a massive skull fracture and blood clot, now complicated by an infection from pneumonia. The doctors know there is no way they can save him.

The Selma Voting Rights Struggle

Meetings and Decisions

TUSKEGEE: After the second march is halted on Turnaround Tuesday, TIAL meets on Tuesday night and decides to hold their Montgomery action the next day regardless. Since the march is blocked in Selma, they will open a "Second Front" of the struggle by marching to the Capitol and delivering to Governor Wallace a freedom petition. Despite opposition from some Tuskegee administrators, donations are collected, buses are chartered, and a car caravan is organized.

SELMA: In the aftermath of the turnaround on the bridge, at roughly the same time as TIAL is committing to march in Montgomery and Rev. Reeb was eating dinner with his companions at Walkers Cafe, a tense meeting begins in Selma between SNCC leaders and SCLC executive staff. It flares into shouting, bitter recriminations, harsh accusations, and open hostility over what happened and what to do next. The confrontation halts only when Rev. Reeb and his bloodied companions stagger into the office.

Learning that students are marching on the morrow in Montgomery, SNCC Executive Secretary Jim Forman decides to pull most of the SNCC staff out of Selma and into Montgomery where Tuskegee and Alabama State College students form a natural SNCC constituency.

Meanwhile, at the evening mass meeting in Brown Chapel, Dr. King calls for a Wednesday morning march to the Dallas County courthouse to pray for Reeb's life, to protest police and Klan violence, and to continue demanding the right to vote.

Wednesday, March 10

NATION: Fueled by the vicious attack on Reeb and the other ministers, mass protests in support of voting rights expand in cities and towns across the nation.

WASHINGTON: Feeling heat from their constituents and tired of waiting for the Justice Department to propose legislation,

The March to Montgomery

senate Republicans and northern Democrats each begin drafting their own (rival) voting bills. Bowing to political reality, the administration shelves the Constitutional amendment approach. They now focus on drafting their own voting rights bill. To achieve a unified, bipartisan bill, Attorney General Katzenbach urgently negotiates with Senate Minority Leader Everett Dirksen (R-IL) whose support is essential for overcoming the inevitable southern filibuster. Then he meets with Senate Majority Leader Mike Mansfield (D-MT). Democrats have a 2-1 majority in the Senate, but the southern wing of the party — the "Dixiecrats" — are bitterly opposed to any legislation that will increase the number of Black voters. (The House does not allow filibustering, and there are enough northern Democrats and sympathetic Republicans to assure passage, so the Senate is where the decisive legislative battle will be fought.)

BLACK BELT: Throughout the period between Turnaround Tuesday and the final March to Montgomery, mass meetings, registration efforts, and protests continue and expand in the rural counties around Selma. Marchers are attacked, tear-gassed, jailed, and beaten by state troopers, local cops and Sheriff Clark's posse in places like Camden (Wilcox County) and elsewhere in the western half of Alabama's Black Belt. Though almost totally ignored by the national news media, these defiant actions have a profound effect on both Blacks *and* whites whose families have lived in these isolated communities for generations — in some cases since slavery days. Though of course they are demonstrating for the right to vote, on a deeper, more fundamental level, the marchers are asserting their human dignity, demanding respect as equal citizens, and by their own actions, ending the culture of forced social subservience. Unnoticed by *The* New York Times and CBS News, Blacks begin to carry themselves with pride instilled by their own raw courage; most local whites, however reluctantly, recognize that though they still retain enormous economic power compared to Blacks, the days of feudal lordship and legally mandated social supremacy are coming to an end.

Coming to an end because Blacks simply won't put up with it any longer.

"The Berlin Wall"

SELMA: On Wednesday morning, Brown Chapel seethes with life, energy, anger, and sorrow. Selma students lead mass singing that rocks the soul. Bulletins from Birmingham charting Rev. Reeb's decline are read from the pulpit. Northern whites and Alabama Blacks enter and leave the church and mill around, mingling and talking while they wait for the prayer-march to the courthouse. With the cops surrounding the Carver Project, and Klansmen and posse prowling the perimeter, the project's tiny candy shack is the only place white supporters can safely buy cigarettes, pop, and other incidentals. The line outside its window is a dozen deep all day long.

SCLC staff member Charles Fager recalled:

> [An] impressive spirit and welcome had been shown by the black community of Selma to the horde of outside visitors which coursed through its mainly dirt streets in these days. Most of the local blacks knew little of white people except what they had learned in the context of the Black Belt's segregated, crazy-quilt class structure; and they were thus amazed and astonished to see first scores, and then hundreds of men and women of the same shade now coming to stand with them as they attempted to make a dent in this system. For years afterward, they would speak of these pilgrims coming as perhaps the most moving aspect of the most vivid period of their lives. And they responded with a rush of hospitality, treating practically every obscure clergyman with a bedroll as if he were a visiting church primate...
>
> Soon enough the benches and floors of Brown Chapel and First Baptist were littered each night after the mass meetings with the tired, uncomfortable bodies of people,

The March to Montgomery

> usually the latest arrivals, trying to sleep as best they could. But this was because almost every house with a spare bed — and many without — had taken in as many of the hundreds of visitors as they could hold. At Good Samaritan Hospital, a wing that had been recently closed was hastily reopened and the floor carpeted with old mattresses; under the attentions of Father Ouellet and Sister Michael Ann, Good Samaritan's administrator, it became a hostel for religious people, particularly the steady stream of Catholic nuns and priests. In their humble houses the hosts plied their guests with the best meals they could afford, and many a stranger developed a lingering taste for collard greens and sweet potato pie in the course of a short stay. At the churches, a corps of intent, perspiring women labored all day and into each night frying heaps of chicken and baking large oblong pans full of warm, crumbly corn bread, for once cooking meals for white folks with all the pride anyone could ask for. — Charles Fager. [10]

At mid-day, Rev. L.L. Anderson of Tabernacle Baptist leads 500 people out of Brown Chapel on a march to the Dallas County courthouse. They barely get out of the church before a line of city cops block their progress on Sylvan Street. Behind them lurk platoons of state troopers, sheriff's deputies, and the posse of volunteer racists in their khaki work clothes and plastic construction helmets. Mayor Smitherman and Chief Baker declare an "emergency ban" on all marches. *"It is too risky under the present circumstances — taking under consideration the facts as they now affect the city,"* explains the Mayor.

What he means — but is politically unwilling to say — is that if any protesters, Black or white, leave the protection of the Carver housing project which surrounds Brown Chapel, Lingo or Clark might order their men to savagely attack them as on Bloody Sunday. And, that the swarm of local and visiting Klansmen are still on the prowl, hungry for more blood after assaulting three "white niggers" the night before. Neither the troopers, nor the

The Selma Voting Rights Struggle

sheriff's deputies, nor the city police can be counted on to restrain them.

Anderson protests this denial of free speech to no avail. Instead of returning to the church, the marchers remain in the street face-to-face with the cops. One by one, local activists and visiting clergy — nuns, ministers, rabbis, priests — loudly address the issues, proclaim their commitment to justice, pray for brotherhood and an end to racism, and demand the right to vote. First to speak is Sister Antona, a Black nun from St. Louis. Interspersed with the speeches are spirited freedom songs led by the young students. Hour after hour the confrontation continues.

Sister Antona is just one of many Black and white Roman Catholic priests and nuns in their distinctive cleric garb. Under the leadership of Father Maurice Ouellet, the Society of St. Edmund has been providing logistical support to SNCC organizers in Selma for more than a year, defying the church hierarchy that has long barred Catholic clergy from participating in the Civil Rights Movement, or for that matter, any other social-justice activity. Now in answer to King's call, a few members of the Catholic clergy are defiantly putting their bodies on the line, face-to-face with the cops — most of them without permission from their superiors and none with the consent of Alabama Bishop Thomas Toolen. In years to come, some of these priests and nuns go on to become active in the Catholic Left and supporters of Liberation Theology, often in opposition to their ecclesiastic superiors.

As the standoff on Sylvan continues, protesters gather in First Baptist at the edge of the Carver Project, half a block from Brown Chapel. From there, 250 marchers try to outflank the cops on Sylvan and reach the courthouse by way of Jefferson Davis Avenue. A car caravan of troopers rushes to head them off. Swinging, poking, and stabbing with their clubs, they drive the demonstrators back into the church.

Outside Brown Chapel, Police Chief Wilson Baker strings a waist-high clothesline across Sylvan Street to mark the line that

The March to Montgomery

marchers are not allowed to pass. The Selma students quickly dub it the "" and they improvise a new freedom song to the tune of "Battle of Jericho:"

> *We've got a rope that's a Berlin Wall,*
>
> *Berlin Wall, Berlin Wall,*
>
> *We've got a rope that's a Berlin Wall,*
>
> *In Selma, Alabama.*
>
> *We're gonna stay here 'till it falls,*
>
> *'till it falls, 'till it falls,*
>
> *We're gonna stay here 'till it falls,*
>
> *In Selma, Alabama.*

It will be six days and nights of around-the-clock, 24-hour vigil in hard cold rain and blazing sun before Selma's "Berlin Wall" finally falls.

As the vigil continues, MCHR doctors Jack Geiger and Richard Hausknecht are nabbed by state troopers who take them to the courthouse where they are grilled by officials of the Alabama Medical Society. State licensing board administrator Douglas Benton threatens them with arrest if they give any kind of first aid to anyone at any time. By way of example, he informs them that if they been present when Rev. Reeb was beaten, they would have been liable for arrest had they done anything to help him. (In fact, Alabama law specifically permits unlicensed doctors to give emergency first-aid, but not, apparently, if the patient is Black or in favor of civil rights.)

Hearing Before Federal Judge Johnson

MONTGOMERY: While student marchers are confronting the "Berlin Wall" in Selma, Dr. King, DCVL, and SCLC

The Selma Voting Rights Struggle

leaders appear before Judge Johnson on Wednesday morning for his hearing on their *Williams v Wallace* petition that the state of Alabama be ordered to allow the march to Montgomery. The courtroom is crowded with supporters and reporters. King is called to the stand and state attorneys try to prove he had violated Johnson's "no-march" injunction the day before. Civil rights attorney and SNCC activist Don Jelinek recalled:

> [Johnson] was the best federal Judge in the entire South on integration. Then he switched over to be the most anti Black-militant judge in the entire zone, and he's the one that caused Dr. King the enormous crisis of the 2nd march [Turnaround Tuesday] when he issued an injunction against them which was outrageous even among the racist judges. He believed in the NAACP Legal Defense Fund approach. He believed you do it lawfully; you do it in stages through the courts. And he was obsessed against anybody that dealt with civil disobedience. ... He thought that Dr. King was a menace to the future of the South becoming an integrated place. That [King] would bring back the torrent of bad feelings, by [not] going slow and NAACP-style legally through the courts. Dr. King was really his greatest enemy until SNCC surpassed King in [Johnson]'s mind.
>
> Dr. King then had to face contempt charges before Judge Johnson. ... [He] wanted Dr. King to be forced to go on the record and talk about the arrangement that had been made with the Justice Dept so as to put a real break between [King] and the other movements. ... discredit him, and also separate him from SNCC and the other groups, knowing the reaction that did occur would occur because Johnson was politically sophisticated. ... And then once King told Johnson what he already knew [about the agreement to turn around at the bridge], then Johnson dismissed the charges and declared him not in contempt.
> — Don Jelinek. [16]

The March to Montgomery

Though Judge Johnson does not jail Dr. King, neither does he issue any ruling on the main issue of the Freedom Movement's right to march to Montgomery. Instead, the hearing runs all day and continues into Thursday. Movement supporters are puzzled at the tedious, lengthy testimony, and some believe that the judge's delaying tactics have more to do with coordinating political strategy with LBJ and Katzenbach than any legal complexities in what is clearly an open and shut First Amendment issue. They suspect that the judge is blocking the march until the administration manages to pull together a voting rights bill and submit it to Congress. Then LBJ can spin the march to Montgomery — when it finally occurs — as a march in support of *his* bill and *his* leadership rather than an indictment of federal indifference, inaction, and complicity with racial segregation.

Students March in Montgomery

MONTGOMERY: Also on Wednesday, March 10, while King is in court and Selma students are being blocked at the "Berlin Wall," more than 700 Tuskegee students board buses and cars to head for Montgomery, just a 45-minute drive east on Highway 80. They carry with them a carefully worded freedom petition they are determined to deliver to Wallace. They also carry brown bag lunches of apples and bologna sandwiches prepared by the Black women who work in the cafeteria.

The cars and buses bring the marchers to First Baptist Church in Montgomery, six blocks from the capitol. This is the famous "brick-a-day" church founded by freed slaves — one of the oldest Black churches in America. Bombed several times by white racists, it was the church where Rev. Abernathy preached during the Montgomery Bus Boycott and where the Freedom Riders were besieged by a racist mob. The Tuskegee students are joined there by protesters from Montgomery, including a number of Alabama State College (ASC) students.

The Selma Voting Rights Struggle

Tuskegee Professor Jean Wiley recalls:

> We're there, there must be 1500 of us, and we realized as soon as we get out of the cars and buses, it was way over our head. ... And we see these people pulling up, and they all have on overalls, and the brogan boots — these folks are ready. Now when you look at the difference between us and them — and I don't see anybody I'm recognizing — and then I realize — then we all realize — this has to be SNCC. ... For me, it was my first time to see SNCC *en masse*. ...
>
> And they are moving, I mean, they are moving. They are real veterans, now. And there are men as well as women, because one of the first women that I tried to talk to is Annie Pearl Avery. And she ain't having it, she's too busy, she's too busy. They're directing people, they're forming the perimeter. They're doing this and that, and they're trying to train [us] in nonviolent action even as we're moving [toward the Capitol], it was extraordinary, it was a wonderful picture. ... It was such a comfort to see the SNCC people, clearly ready to — because we could see the troopers amassing and the cops, they were quite visible and they were not in small numbers. ... So SNCC people are talking with authority. This is what you do, this is how you secure the perimeter, this is how you do this, this is how you move as opposed to just straggling along up to the Capitol ... — Jean Wiley, TIAL and later SNCC. [16]

While some of the SNCC staff march with the Tuskegee students toward the Capitol, other SNCC members head for all-Black Alabama State College to mobilize additional support. When the march reaches the Capitol building — the "Cradle of the Confederacy" — cops block them on Dexter Avenue at the foot of the long flight of steps leading up to the colonnade entrance. A contingent of state troopers who have been drawn off from the

The March to Montgomery

swarm occupying Selma, line up to prevent anyone from stepping on the Capitol grounds, which is state property.

TIAL leaders attempt to see Governor Wallace who refuses to meet with them or accept their petition. For some of the student leaders — future Black ministers, lawyers and doctors — being treated, *"no different from other Black people, the country people, the people of Selma, anywhere,"* comes as a shock. Those who have been working with SNCC are not surprised. State troopers swing their clubs to prevent Blacks from stepping on the sacred soil of state property. Meanwhile, Montgomery police surround the marchers on the city street.

> When police officers' billy clubs battered the heads of several students, the students immediately sat down in the streets and sang freedom songs. The ridin' on high to freedom had plummeted to the sinkin' on low of what it means to be Black in Alabama. The moral purity of the students' purpose, protected by their enthusiastic singing of freedom songs, warded off the enveloping gloom that Black people's freedom was not on Alabama's agenda. The actions of the FBI left us wondering if we, as a people, were even on the nation's agenda. — Gwen Patton, TIAL leader. [18]

TIAL leaders George Ware, George Davis and Bill Hall try to read the petition aloud to the press. They are arrested. Now sitting on the pavement and surrounded by city cops and state troopers, the marchers hold their ground. The police assure them that if they leave the sit-in to obtain water or use restrooms they will be allowed to rejoin the demonstration. But when they try to do so, they are barred from returning to the group.

The worst moment for me comes late in the afternoon, when several squadrons of [possemen] on horseback move to a triangular attack position and threaten to charge if we don't leave. The SNCC people order all women on the ground, hands covering their heads. Mind you, some of those doing the ordering

The Selma Voting Rights Struggle

are themselves women, seasoned veterans of many civil rights battles. I feel both shock and relief at seeing them among the men.

> Now, there is no question in my mind that the horses will charge, but this is an order I cannot follow. After all, these are my young students, whom I'd worked hard to get here. I'm the one who should be protecting them — the young men as well as the women. Somebody points and yells at me to get down. As I'm trying to explain, somebody else throws me to the ground, where I lie terrified and helpless, surrounded by the sounds of snorting, stomping horses, and cursing armed white men. — Jean Wiley. [17]

The Montgomery County's mounted sheriff's posse does not charge the sitting students, and there is no large-scale attack as occurred in Marion or Selma. In part this is because they are under the eyes of reporters and cameras, and in part because Tuskegee is an internationally-known institution with many of its students coming from prominent and politically powerful Black families in the North as well as the South.

> One interesting thing for me was the long-standing class division between Tuskegee and Alabama State. That was something nobody liked to talk about, but it was there, and you saw it just fall apart. That distinction just fell apart, because when Tuskegee students were locked inside the perimeter, it was the Alabama State students who came [in support] and therefore they were among the first to get arrested because they were trying to get in to help the Tuskegee students, and hundreds of them got arrested. — Jean Wiley. [16]

As more and more ASC students and local community people arrive to support the protest, the cops keep them on the periphery and prevent from joining the sit-in. Though the Tuskegee students are spared the worst of police savagery, out of the media's sight, cops rampage through the Black neighborhood, beating heads,

The March to Montgomery

breaking through doors, harassing and threatening any Afro man or woman they encounter.

By late afternoon the demonstrators — Tuskegee and ASC students and Montgomery residents — still hold their ground, but the day is growing late and the buses are scheduled to return to Tuskegee. More than 500 leave the street sit-in and head back to Tuskegee to continue the struggle on campus. But a hard core of several hundred refuse to move. As night falls, they continue to occupy a portion of the pavement at the foot of the Capitol steps, singing freedom songs and speaking truth about Black and white in Alabama.

> And that's when [SNCC leader James] Forman started the "Toilet Revolution" [AKA the "Great Pee-In"]. Okay, people had to go to the bathroom and … Jim says: "Well just do it here." And we just pissed, and it ran right down the hill. It actually was a "toilet" revolution, we peed down the hill from the Capitol. — Hardy Frye, SNCC. [16]

After midnight, a cold, drenching rain sweeps across the Alabama Black Belt. In Selma, the protesters holding the line at the "Berlin Wall" can obtain umbrellas and winter coats from home and rig light plastic tarps for shelter, but when the Tuskegee students left campus for what they assumed would be a few hours in Montgomery, the weather had been mild. They are still dressed in shirtsleeves or thin sweaters and the cops prevent anyone from bringing them foul-weather gear. Soaked and shivering, the students retreat, seeking shelter in Dexter Avenue Baptist Church a block away. Dexter had been Dr. King's church during the Montgomery Bus Boycott until he later moved to Atlanta. As is normal for Black churches in that era, the doors are not locked, but the church deacons are furious when they discover that the students have moved in without asking their permission.

> The students sought refuge at the nearby Dexter Avenue Baptist Church, the famed Black church where Dr.

Martin Luther King, Jr., pastored, just one block from the State Capitol. It was after midnight. Exhausted and chilled to the bone, students sought sleep on the floor, in the pews wherever they could lie down to rest. The toilets would not flush; there was no water; there was no heat; there were no lights; the Deacon Board had had the utilities cut off. Outside, the law enforcers encircled the church ... — Dr. Gwen Patton. [18]

Thursday, March 11

NATION: Demonstrations supporting Black voting rights continue across the country. In city after city, civil rights organizations — particularly CORE — organize street marches and sit-in occupations of federal buildings. In churches and on college campuses, Friends of SNCC chapters mobilize support and collect money, books, food, and clothing for the Alabama Black Belt. Telegrams are flooding Congress and phones are ringing off the hook. Do something! Do something now!

WASHINGTON: Twelve students, Black and white, pose as tourists and slip into the White House where they stage a main-corridor sit-in. The first (and so far as is known, the only) such protest ever to occur inside the White House itself. They remain all day. But in the evening there is a swank soiree for members of Congress and their wives. Such notables might be offended by the sight of American citizens exercising their Free Speech rights about an issue that is shaking the nation. The protesters are arrested.

Meanwhile, negotiations for a single bipartisan voting bill continue. Katzenbach, Justice Department lawyers, Senate leaders both Republican and Democrat, Senate staff, and civil rights leaders are all involved to one degree or another. LBJ is pushing them to move fast. By the weekend he wants to announce that he is submitting a bill to Congress.

The March to Montgomery

MONTGOMERY: The injunction hearing before Judge Johnson drones on — and on — and on. It is continued over to Friday.

SELMA: The "Berlin Wall" vigil continues around the clock in intermittent rain. Tired of hearing the protesters sing *"We've got a rope that's a Berlin Wall,"* Chief Baker removes the clothesline barrier (though not his cops). Everyone continues to sing "Berlin Wall" anyway. Several times a day, students try to find a way to march out of the Carver Project, but each time speeding caravans of cars filled with troopers manage to block them.

Confrontation at Dexter Church

MONTGOMERY: As Thursday morning dawns, the hard core of SNCC, Tuskegee and ASC protesters are still holed up in Dexter Avenue Baptist church. They are joined by some northern students and clergy, mostly white, who had been on their way to Selma. SCLC leader Jim Bevel arrives to oppose continuation of the Montgomery protests. Refusing to accept that the Tuskegee students decided on their own to march in Montgomery, he views their actions as a SNCC ploy to undercut and draw attention away from the SCLC-led events in Selma. The students and SNCC staff fiercely refute that, and they blame SCLC for the deacons of Dexter and other churches trying to deny them sanctuary from storm and police the night before. To them, that's a fundamental violation of everything the Freedom Movement stands for. SCLC denies they had anything to do with the deacons locking their churches against the students. The deacons are a law unto themselves, and in fact, they're also refusing to allow SCLC to hold meetings in those same churches.

> Wazir Peacock of SNCC — At this point, Jim Forman had been with us ... [SCLC] attacked him and all that, and since we didn't budge, they really got nasty with him. They wanted to put it on him that he was the cause of it, as if no way overnight we [students] could get

that strong in our conviction to do what we did [on our own]. But TIAL had been organized before, maybe in the summer or fall of '64, It was reactivated, they reactivated it. It wasn't a new student activist organization — it wasn't new. [16]

Charles Fager of SCLC — The demonstrations in Montgomery have been marked by conflict, between SNCC and SCLC staff and between SNCC and local black preachers. SCLC wants to keep control of the actions mounted in support of the Selma campaign, particularly those during these days when the voting bill was being drafted and Judge Frank Johnson was deliberating over whether to permit the march to proceed. The local black ministers in Montgomery were almost unanimously staying away from both organizations and the campaign. This attitude had much to do with the failure of Dr. King's effort to mount a large march on the registrars' office there in February. Both SNCC and SCLC had great difficulty in finding a pastor in the city willing to allow mass meetings to be held in his church... [10]

Jean Wiley, TIAL — Part of this, we're all novices here, you know, and for almost all of the students, this is their first time to do any direct action of any kind, so they're raring to go. I'm not sure we even talked about, or tried to organize any support. We knew a lot of Tuskegee students had relatives, like Gwen [Patton] herself, in Montgomery. We had no way of knowing that the churches wouldn't be supportive, I mean, that never crossed anybody's mind. And we also thought that being in Montgomery would force some action from Selma. We thought being there would help to get the march going in another direction, although we have no word from SCLC about anything except you can't use the churches, that's the only word we got from them. [16]

The March to Montgomery

The argument grows loud and heated, accusations and insults are shouted back and forth. It becomes so angry that Forman and Bevel appear to be on the verge physically attacking each other. Forman cuts it short by announcing he is going back to the Capitol to resume the protest. But the church is surrounded by cops who immediately arrest him and the SNCC members who follow him out the door, dragging them off to jail on unspecified charges. When Bevel tries to leave for Selma, he too is arrested, ending up in the cell next to Forman. When the mass of several hundred protesters attempt to exit the church, the police beat them back inside.

Death of Rev. Reeb

BIRMINGHAM: All day Wednesday and into Thursday, Rev. Reeb's condition slowly deteriorates in a Birmingham hospital. The doctors know it is just a matter of time.

For the national media, the attack on the white ministers and news of Reeb's medical condition are major stories that equal, or surpass, the Turnaround Tuesday events on the bridge. Both stories continue to clash with President Johnson's, "Defend Democracy in Vietnam" PR campaign. He is not amused.

For Blacks, the contrast between the public reaction to the murder of Jimmie Lee Jackson and the assault on Reeb is stark and bitter. Senators, congressional representatives, and other prominent Americans send personal telegrams of concern and condolence to Reeb's home in Boston. Pundits comment and analyze at length, and when Mrs. Reeb flies to Birmingham, she has to dodge a swarm of reporters to reach her husband's side. For Mrs. Jackson, there had been nothing; not a note, not a phone call, and at most a few lines in the national press. Most galling of all is that the white public in general does not even notice the discrepancy; to them the police murder of an Afro man is of no consequence. But Black bitterness is not directed against Rev. Reeb — the people in Selma know he put his life in danger to stand with them and they honor and respect him for his courage and support.

The Selma Voting Rights Struggle

Shortly before 7 pm Thursday, March 11, Rev. Reeb dies. President Johnson phones Mrs. Reeb in Birmingham and arranges to fly her and her husband's body home on an Air Force jet.

SELMA: Police Chief Wilson Baker announces that he knows the identities of the four killers, and he promises to file murder charges against them. Meanwhile, the "Berlin Wall" vigil continues around the clock in a cold rain. Squads and platoons of cops and troopers face the nonviolent protesters, determined to prevent any marching anywhere. From behind the police lines, white thugs hurl rocks at the nonviolent protesters, hoping to provoke some response that the cops can use as an excuse for an attack. On one occasion, they even fire a pistol, lightly wounding a teenage girl. As usual, all the forces of law and order gathered in their hundreds — local, state, and federal — ignore these acts of violence by whites against Blacks.

Four white men are eventually indicted for murdering Rev. Reeb. One of them, R.B Kelley, provides information to the police and is never brought to court. In December of 1965, the other three, Elmer Cook, William Hoggle and Namon "Duck" Hoggle are put on trial in Selma. They are quickly acquitted by an all-white jury. The courtroom is packed with white spectators who greet the verdict with applause and cheers. No federal charges are ever filed against the four killers. In March 2011, 46 years later, the FBI announces it is reopening the case as a Civil Rights era "cold-case" investigation.

Friday, March 12 – Sunday, March 14

WASHINGTON: While protests roil the streets of Washington and elsewhere around the country, on Friday, intense negotiations over voting rights language between Senate kingpins, administration officials and civil rights principals continue. By now legislative leaders agree that some provision for suspending the so-called "literacy tests" must be included in the bill and also authority to send federal registrars into counties that continue to systematically deny Black voting

The March to Montgomery

rights. But there is no agreement on the formulas or thresholds that would trigger such "drastic" federal action. (By some, no doubt odd coincidence, none of the formulas proposed by Johnson appointees would apply to conditions in Texas.) Another thorny issue is just how strong federal oversight of election and registration procedures should be in the affected states and counties, and whether all poll taxes should be eliminated.

MONTGOMERY: Meanwhile, Judge Johnson's marathon hearing on the right of American citizens to march in protest and petition their Governor for redress of grievances drags on — and on — and on. At the end of the day, it's continued over to Monday, March 15.

On Friday evening, the students still holding out at Dexter Church vote to return to their colleges where they can mobilize for further action come Monday. Jim Forman of SNCC issues a national call for students — many of whom are now on Spring break — to converge on Montgomery to support the protests. A truckload of supplies including helmets, tents, sleeping bags, and cooking gear is purchased. Some SNCC members disagree with Forman's strategy of mounting large-scale protests in Montgomery. They argue that media-oriented demonstrations are SCLC's way, not SNCC's, and that SNCC should stick to deep-roots organizing.

SELMA: The "Berlin Wall" vigil continues — around the clock in a cold rain. From before dawn to deep in the night the women in the church kitchens continue to serve fried chicken, greens, and cornbread to hungry protesters who grab a few winks of sleep on the church pews between mass meetings and their shift on the line. All of the women laboring at the hot stoves hour after hour are Black — except one. Nellie Washburn is the daughter of Nannie Washburn — 65 years old, Georgia born, child of white sharecroppers, a textile worker from age 7, a union organizer in the 1930s, a life-long "Red," and a stalwart opponent of racism and exploitation. She, her blind son, Joe, and her daughter Nellie answered Dr. King's call.

The Selma Voting Rights Struggle

> Well, ... my daughter, son, and I refused to eat the Jim Crow food, because there wasn't anybody in the kitchen a cookin' except black women that was older than ... as old as I was, and I was sixty-five. ... I went to Rev. Hollis and asked him. I said, "We not gonna eat ya Jim Crow food." And he says, "Why?" I said, ... "My daughter has droved us, my son and I, down here, and I didn't think I'd come to a Jim Crow kitchen." And he said, "You a guest." I said, "No, I'm not. I just one of 'em." And he said then, "I don't know nothin' we could do about it." I says, "Well, don't you think the black women's been in the kitchen too long cookin' for the white people?" And he commenced studyin', and he said, "The only thing I can do is to let yo'r daughter go in the kitchen. I wouldn't let you." You know, I was sixty- five. — Nannie Washburn. [15]

Later, on the final March to Montgomery, Nannie and her son walk the entire 54 miles. Afterward, as an LPN, she is asked to become part of the MCHR medical team in Alabama. In Demopolis (Marengo County) where her son is arrested and viciously abused in jail, she works at the MCHR aid station, treating victims of tear gas and billy clubs. The church is surrounded by cops to blockade them. Inside, they sleep with the lights off because of Klan snipers. Nannie is arrested on vague charges. The authorities decide that she's insane for associating with and supporting Blacks. Without trial, they incarcerate her in the state mental institution in Tuscaloosa for 21 days before Movement lawyers can finally free her.

NATION: On Saturday and Sunday, weekend demonstrations in support of voting rights flare in cities large and small across the nation. Some 30,000 people march in New York, half up 5th Avenue and the other half in Harlem, led by nuns from the Sisters of Charity. John Lewis, Jim Forman, and Bayard Rustin address the New York rallies. Two marches are also held in San Francisco, one a long torchlight parade that snakes through the city. In Los Angeles, students block mail trucks to protest federal inaction. More than 20,000 participate in a "Rally for Freedom" on Boston Common, and 10,000 defiantly march in New Orleans past angry white crowds who heckle and threaten them. Protests of varying sizes are held in other urban centers, and also in places like Norfolk VA, Binghamton NY, St. Augustine FL, and Bakersfield CA. In San Jose CA and Beloit WI marchers set off on 54-mile treks — the same distance as from Selma to Montgomery. And in Ottawa Canada and other foreign capitols there are sympathy protests outside American embassies.

WASHINGTON: More than 15,000 rally in Lafayette Park across from the White House where Fannie Lou Hamer tells them: "It's time now to stop begging them for what should have been done 100 years ago. We have stood up on our feet, and God knows we're on our way!" Close by, more than 1,000 people picket around the clock on Pennsylvania Avenue, their songs and chants clearly audible inside the West Wing corridors of power where Katzenbach tells LBJ that negotiating and drafting the voting rights bill is almost complete. It will be ready for submission on Monday. Johnson announces to the press that on Monday evening he will present the bill to Congress in a nationally televised address.

Monday, March 15

BLACK BELT: Monday is one of the two days per month when voters are allowed to register. In the counties surrounding Selma where the voting rights movement has taken wing, the familiar pattern is repeated. If Blacks go to the courthouse alone or in small groups, they are vulnerable to violent Klan ambush, police harassment, and arrest on trumped up charges; if they march together for safety, they risk being accused of "parading without a permit," mass arrest, tear gas, charging horses, and billy-clubs. Those who do reach the court house to register are confronted with delaying tactics, trickery, the so-called "literacy test," and the requirement that an already-registered voter "vouch" for them.

The Selma Voting Rights Struggle

LOWNDES COUNTY: In "Bloody Lowndes" County, no church dares open its doors for a freedom meeting. Black families fear to take in a civil rights "agitator" for an overnight stay — and with good reason. Everyone knows that the heavily armed Klansmen who surrounded Mount Carmel church on the mere rumor that they might be talking about voting would immediately assassinate the freedom worker and lynch whoever provided housing. So SNCC and SCLC field organizers are limited to brief, stealthy, day trips from Selma. That does not mean nothing is happening. Hidden from view like a smoldering ember beneath dry leaves, the freedom fire is slowly catching hold in Lowndes. On the previous registration day two weeks earlier, John Hulett and a courageous, self-organized band of 37 went to the courthouse in Hayneville to register. Carl Golson, the Registrar of Voters, tricked them into walking miles in the cold rain to a phony location. Now, more than 20 of them return to the courthouse and again ask to register.

This time Golson sends them to the old, long-abandoned county jail. Inside is an ancient indoor gallows with a noose still hanging from the arm. *"I wonder if that ol' thing still works,"* a deputy sheriff mutters ominously. One by one, the Black applicants have to go in alone to fill out the registration forms and take the test. The official performs his duties at a leisurely pace with frequent rest breaks. Only 17 of the 20 manage to complete the process before closing. Weeks later, they learn that 15 of them "failed" the test. But two — John Hulett and John Lawson — become the first Black voters in "Bloody" Lowndes County since the late 1800s. No one believes that their successful attempt to register indicates any softening of white supremacy. Rather the assumption is that the power structure simply got tired of news stories reporting that there's not a single Black voter in the entire county. Now there are two.

MONTGOMERY: Meanwhile, the hearing before Judge Johnson begins its fourth day of examining the seemingly complex question of whether American citizens should be allowed to peacefully march to their state capitol and petition for redress of grievances (as is plainly and explicitly permitted by the First Amendment to the United States Constitution). Once again, the hearing is continued over to the following day, but this time with a significant change. The judge instructs the SCLC lawyers to prepare and present detailed plans for their proposed march to Montgomery — a sign that he intends to rule in favor of the march. While Movement observers are elated, some note that this forward motion in the long-stalled proceeding takes place only after President Johnson is finally ready to submit his voting bill to Congress with a televised address to the nation on the issue of Black voting rights. LBJ can now spin the March to Montgomery as support for *his* leadership and *his* legislation.

Protests and Police Violence Continue

MONTGOMERY: Also on Monday, Jim Forman and SNCC staff lead 400 or so Alabama State students on a march from the ASC campus to the Capitol a dozen blocks away. Joining them are a number of mostly white northern students who have responded to Forman's call. Halfway there, cops block them at Jackson and High streets in the heart of the Black community. College administrators try to talk the protesters into returning to school, but the students refuse. Local Blacks urge the young marchers to hold fast.

Jackson and High is a center of Black commerce. On one corner is the Ben Moore hotel, Black-built, Black-owned, and the only hotel in the city where Blacks are welcome to stay. It was a hub of activity during the Montgomery Bus Boycott, and over the years has become the usual site of the rare meetings between white and Black community leaders (because, of course, it is unthinkable for white officials to meet with Blacks in City Hall as if they were equal citizens). SNCC now uses the hotel as their unofficial headquarters, the place where they hold staff and strategy meetings.

The demonstrators are blocked in the Jackson and High district for most of the afternoon, but as evening falls, the police line is

The Selma Voting Rights Struggle

withdrawn and they resume marching toward the Alabama seat of government. As they near the Capitol, they are surrounded and attacked by state troopers and sheriff's deputies mounted on horses.

Meanwhile, back at the Jackson and High commercial district, the Montgomery County sheriff's posse, some of them mounted, show up eager for action. As a center of Black business and political activity, the district is a tempting target. Finding no marchers to attack, they beat local Blacks and charge against them with their horses. Not part of an organized demonstration, and with no defined leadership, the community responds with thrown rocks, bottles, and bricks. In retaliation the possemen escalate their violence.

Reeb Memorial March in Selma

SELMA: The voter registration process in Dallas County is now partly governed by federal court injunction. Black voter applicants are allowed into the courthouse to apply in the order they are listed in the appearance book — but few are actually registered.

Back on Wednesday, March 10th, the march to the Dallas County courthouse to pray for Rev. Reeb was blocked by the "Berlin Wall." On this Monday, six days later, the vigil still continues around the clock, day after day, in sun and rain, though the goal now is to hold a courthouse memorial service rather than pray for Reeb's recovery. But still they are barred by the forces of "law and order" — Selma city cops, sheriff's deputies and possemen, and Alabama State Troopers. State alcohol agents and game wardens wearing green plastic helmets have been called in to replace troopers who were shifted to Montgomery in response to the student-led "second front."

Rachel West, age 8, remembers:

> During that time, it seemed each day and each night was like the one before it; nothing changed. The rope stayed

The March to Montgomery

there, we stayed there, the troopers stayed there; we'd sing hour after hour until our throats became hoarse. The rain fell, fell almost constantly. The sun would come out briefly, then it would start raining again. We'd be soaked to the skin. It would turn warm; it would turn cold. — Rachel West. [9]

With the march blocked, the Freedom Movement assembles for a Reeb memorial in a jam-packed Brown Chapel. Dr. King is scheduled to deliver the eulogy, but he is stuck in Montgomery at Judge Johnson's interminable injunction hearing. The hours tick by and the crowd grows restless, even annoyed, at the delay. Late in the afternoon, King arrives and is ushered to the podium.

Dr. King's eulogy for Rev. Reeb evokes memories of the Birmingham children and Jimmy Lee Jackson. He places Reeb's murder in context, laying blame not just on the *"sick, misguided"* killers, but also on indifferent religious leaders and irrelevant churches that *"keep silent behind the safe security of stained glass windows."* He condemns the *"timidity"* of the federal government and the apathy of citizens it supposedly serves. And, *"Yes, he was murdered even by the cowardice of every Negro who tacitly accepts the evil of segregation."* He goes on to talk about the Freedom Movement and what it means, recalling the Montgomery Bus Boycott, the student sit-ins, and the Freedom Rides.

Dr. King ends his eulogy with a testimony of hope. He tells the story of Bus Boycott's darkest hour, of how he was sitting in a courtroom where an Alabama judge was about to issue an injunction shutting down the carpools upon which the boycott depended. *"The clock said it was noon, but it was midnight in my soul."* Then, suddenly, news arrived that the United States Supreme Court had ruled against bus segregation. *"Out of the wombs of a frail world, new systems of equality and justice are being born..."* There are seeds of hope for, *"the shirtless and barefoot people. ... Therefore, I am not yet discouraged about the future ... So we thank God for the life of James Reeb. We thank

The Selma Voting Rights Struggle

God for his goodness." [8]

As Dr. King finishes, Rev. Abernathy rushes into the church and comes to the podium to announce that the "Berlin Wall" has fallen! Federal Judge Thomas in Mobile has issued an injunction permitting a march to the courthouse and a memorial service on the steps. The judge's ruling is the result of behind the scenes maneuvering and complex negotiations among Movement leaders and visiting religious dignitaries, Leroy Collins of the Federal Community Relations Service, and Selma Police Chief Wilson Baker who, for days, has argued in vain with Sheriff Clark to allow a memorial march and end the exhausting stand-off.

A wave euphoria sweeps through the packed church. The crowd surges through the doors and out on to Sylvan Street where they begin forming a march line three abreast. Angrily, grudgingly, the cops and possemen and troopers grip their billy clubs and step reluctantly to the side. More than 3,500 strong, the marchers stride down Sylvan Street, swelling with pride and "an immense sense of accomplishment" as they pass the spot where, for so long, they have been blocked. Under the strict terms of the injunction, the protesters are not allowed to gather for the service, so only those at the front of the line can hear the brief prayer and Dr. King's short tribute to all those who have been killed struggling for freedom. When they conclude by singing *We Shall Overcome,* everyone lifts their voices. The song flows like a wave back down the line that stretches for blocks along Alabama Avenue. As they head back to Brown Chapel, the line turns at the courthouse so that every single marcher, Black and white, shares in the small victory of reaching the courthouse steps.

For the Freedom Movement, the courthouse march is an encouraging win. And with the "Berlin Wall" now broken, there is no need to resume the vigil. The daily mass meetings continue, filled with fervor and expectation as Selma Blacks and outside supporters await President Johnson's speech and Judge Johnson's ruling on the injunction. The city police return to their normal duties and the possemen bitterly slink away, their sense of defeat palpable. The state troopers remain nearby to prevent any attempt to cross the bridge, but they too sense that the tide is turning.

President Johnson: "We Shall Overcome"

WASHINGTON: In a televised address to the nation, President Johnson presents the draft Voting Rights Act to a joint session of Congress. Every single senator and representative from Mississippi and Virginia boycott the session as do other southern members. His speech is titled, "The American Promise," and in it, he forthrightly condemns the denial of fundamental rights based on race and the nation's failure to live up to the promise of its creed. Equating the voting rights struggle in Selma with the historic events at Lexington, Concord and Appomattox, Johnson places the issue of equal rights for Blacks at the heart of the nation's purpose to build a society where all men are created equal, and government is by consent of the governed. "There is no Negro problem, there is only an American problem, and we are met here tonight as Americans ... to solve that problem. ... it is not just Negroes, but really it's all of us who must overcome the crippling legacy of bigotry and injustice. And—we—shall—overcome."

Johnson's adoption of the Freedom Movement's signature catch-phrase astonishes both Congress and the nation. Liberals like Emanuel Celler (D-NY) applaud loudly while southern conservatives like Sam Ervin (D-NC) scowl with their arms folded. An estimated 70 million Americans listen to the President's address, none more intently than the freedom soldiers fighting what almost amounts to a second civil war in the Black Belt of Alabama.

> ... we listened to Lyndon Johnson make what many others and I consider not only the finest speech of his career, but probably the strongest speech any American president has ever made on the subject of civil rights. ... I was deeply moved. Lyndon Johnson was no politician that night. He was a man who spoke from his heart. His

were the words of a statesman and more, they were the words of a poet. Dr. King must have agreed. He wiped away a tear at the point where Johnson said the words, "We shall overcome." — John Lewis, SNCC. [11]

MONTGOMERY: But not everyone shares that view. In Montgomery, the SNCC and student demonstrators are still trapped and surrounded by police on a dark street near the Capitol. They listen to LBJ's speech on a tiny transistor radio held aloft in a protester's hand. For some SNCC field secretaries who have endured years of federal indifference, liberal betrayal, and Washington complicity with segregation, the words of LBJ ring hollow and his hypocrisy is unbearable.

> To us, they were tinkling, empty symbols. Johnson also spoiled a good song that day, for to sing "We Shall Overcome" after that speech was to reawaken the sense of hypocrisy created by his use of the three words. — James Forman, SNCC. [19]

SELMA: Yet to the embattled men, women, and children of Alabama's Black Belt, Johnson's speech is a ringing endorsement of their courage and struggle. And it's a promise that their suffering and sacrifice will not be in vain.

> I remember lying on the living room floor in front of the set, watching, listening. It seemed he was speaking directly to me. "The effort of American Negroes to secure for themselves the full blessing of American life must be our cause, too. Because it is not just Negroes, but really, it is all of us who must overcome the crippling legacy of bigotry and injustice. And we shall overcome." When he said that all the people in the room, my sisters, my parents, the ministers, all cried out and applauded. I just lay there watching, listening. Somebody had heard us. ... Except for that one time, we just listened quietly. Once in a while I'd hear my mother or father agree with an, "Um-hmm," but that was all. I remember after his speech going over to Sheyann's, and she was just sitting

there in the living room, thinking about it. And I said, "You hear that speech?" And she says, "I heard it." Then after a long time she said, "But he's there in Washington, and we be down here by ourselves." — Rachel West, Selma student, 8 years old. [9]

Tuesday, March 16

MONTGOMERY: In Judge Johnson's courtroom, SCLC lawyers submit a detailed proposal for a march to Montgomery under federal protection. Unknown to them, the judge has received a personal phone call from U.S. Attorney General Katzenbach. No one knows what was said between them, but now, suddenly, after days of delay, the judge is begins moving with alacrity. Rather than taking days to ponder the imponderable, he ends the session by announcing he will hand down his ruling on the morrow.

Brutal Attack in Montgomery

MONTGOMERY: Jackson Street Baptist Church is the only church in Montgomery willing to open its doors for a SNCC-led protest. On Tuesday morning, more than a thousand demonstrators assemble there for a march on the Capitol in support of voting rights. Many were among the group surrounded by cops the previous evening before being allowed to disperse to their homes and campuses. Others have come from Tuskegee and Alabama State, or are local high school youth cutting class to march for freedom. Also present are some clergy and several hundred northern students, mostly white, who have responded to Forman's call.

As the march approaches the Capitol, Forman and several others advance ahead of the main line to reconnoiter. Suddenly, the Montgomery County mounted posse led by Sheriff Mac Sim Butler charge into them, whips and lariats lashing, long-clubs swinging hard. To keep from being knocked down and trampled

The Selma Voting Rights Struggle

by the hooves of rearing and lunging horses, Forman and the others wrap their arms around light poles, enduring the blows on their backs.

A posseman dressed in green clothes and a white 10-gallon hat stepped up on foot and while the horses partly hid him from view, began clubbing the demonstrators. Several still refused to move, and the man's nightstick began falling with great force on their heads. There was a moment of freakish near-quiet as yells all seemed to subside at once, and in that instant the man in green struck hard on the head of the young man. The sound of the nightstick carried up and down the block. — Roy Reed, New York Times, March 17, 1965.

Forman recalls: "That day became, for me, the last time I wanted to participate in a nonviolent demonstration. ... My ability to continue engaging in nonviolent direct action snapped that day and my anger at the executive branch of the federal government intensified." [19]

Now joined by mounted troopers and sheriff's deputies on foot, the possemen attack the larger group at Decatur and Adams, a few blocks from the Capitol. They violently charge into the marchers, scattering them, driving them back into the Black neighborhood. MCHR doctors Richard Weinerman, Les Falk, Douglas Thompson, and others try to give first aid to the injured. Nurse Robert Dannenburg is arrested and hauled off to the slammer.

In Atlanta, sketchy reports begin coming in over the long-distance WATS line: ... Melzetta Poole, 19, Alabama State, hit in head ... Eric Stern, U. of Pitt., possible broken jaw ... Fran Lipton, U. of Michigan, horse kicked her. ... Rev. Gerald Win, 28, Huntington, Pa ...

> I came to that march with a group from Pittsburgh, PA (3 chartered buses) with a contingent of students, some 30 strong, from the small, liberal arts, Catholic college where I was teaching at the time (Mount Mercy Col-

> lege, since renamed Carlow College). The march never made it to the Capitol building. A few blocks away the police stopped us and surrounded us. ... Suddenly we heard a loud noise coming from a side street ahead of us. A mounted posse came charging around the corner, the police stepped back, and the members of the posse charged into the marchers, clubbing them as they rode through the crowd. Marchers who fled onto porches found themselves trapped as the horse riders came up onto the porches after them. Eventually we made our way back to the church where the march began. — Sam Carcione. [16]

This is not the first time that Sheriff Butler's Montgomery posse has run wild against nonviolent protesters or the Black community — they had done so just the day before in the Jackson and High commercial district. But this time they do it in full view of the national press.

The savage attack with charging horses finally loosens the tight grip Montgomery ministers and deacons have held on their churches. That evening SCLC is able to secure a location for a large mass meeting where the topic is voting rights and police violence. Attending are King, Abernathy, Lewis, Forman, and dozens of local ministers and deacons. Forman's speech is filled with fury, stunning the crowd. As John Lewis recalled, it was, *"One of the angriest, most fiery speeches made by a movement leader up to that point."*

> There's only one man in the country that can stop George Wallace and those posses. These problems will not be solved until the man in that shaggedy old place called the White House begins to shake and gets on the phone and says, "Now listen, George, we're coming down there and throw you in jail if you don't stop that mess." ... I said it today, and I will say it again. If we can't sit at the table of democracy, we'll knock the fucking legs off! — James Forman. [11]

Forman immediately catches himself and apologizes for his profanity in a church before women and children, and he adds the qualification, *"But before we tear it completely down, they will move to build a better one rather than see it destroyed."* He goes on to question the sincerity of LBJ's promises, and in an echo of the original Alabama Project plan drafted by Diane Nash and James Bevel, he calls for, *"tying up every street and bus and committing every act of civil disobedience ever seen because I'm tired of seeing people get hit."* [10]

Though Forman apologizes, many in the church are offended by his language. Some are also alienated by his rage — but others share it. When Dr. King rises to speak, he preaches dedicated nonviolence and steadfast determination in the cause of freedom. *"I'm not satisfied as long as the Negro sees life as a long and empty corridor with a 'no exit' sign at the end. The cup of endurance has run over. ... We cannot stand idly by and allow this to happen. [Tomorrow] we must get together a peaceful and orderly march on the courthouse in Montgomery [to confront Sheriff Butler]."* [10]

Wednesday, March 17

NATION: National TV news on Tuesday night provides vivid images of Sheriff Butler's brutal assault on nonviolent demonstrators, and in northern newspapers on Wednesday morning, it's a page one story. *The New York Times* runs two front-page photos, one of which shows Butler on his charging horse clubbing the head of a fleeing marcher. The *Washington Post* runs eleven separate reports on the attack.

In front of the White House, some 300 SNCC protesters endure snow and freezing temperatures to stage a frigid, sidewalk-sit-in. In Selma, some 600 people, local and northern, hold a protest prayer-service in drenching rain and pounding hail.

The March to Montgomery

Mass March to Montgomery Courthouse

MONTGOMERY: On Wednesday afternoon, Dr. King and Rev. Abernathy of SCLC, and James Forman and Silas Norman of SNCC lead some 2,000 people in pouring rain on a mile-long march from Jackson Street Baptist to the Montgomery County courthouse where Sheriff Butler has his offices. The route requires them to traverse a white neighborhood where furious hecklers line the street, shouting obscenities and curses, throwing what they can find at the protesters. King is their chief target. Alabama State and local high school students surround him in a living shield to protect him. Smarting from national condemnation, on this day the forces of "law and order" choose not to attack. A city official offers a lame apology for the previous day's brutality, *"We are sorry there was a mix-up and a misunderstanding of orders."* Activists assume that "mix-up" and "misunderstanding" refer to brutalizing nonviolent marchers where newsmen could take photos instead of herding the reporters away or waiting for nightfall.

King, Abernathy, Forman, and local Black leaders go inside to meet with Sheriff Butler, city and county officials, and John Doar of the Justice Department. For three long hours, the crowd waits in the rain, singing freedom songs, listening to impromptu speeches, and "testifying." To everyone's astonishment, the city police actually protect the crowd from a menacing throng of white hecklers.

The negotiators finally emerge at dusk. As does Sheriff Butler who apologizes for his posse's violent attacks. The Black leaders announce that white officials have agreed to stop using the posse against protesters. They have also agreed to establish policies and procedures for obtaining march permits to ensure First Amendment freedom of speech rights for Blacks. (The agreement only applies to the Montgomery city streets, not to state property under the jurisdiction of the Alabama State Troopers.) To most of the marchers, face-to-face negotiations between Black leaders and the white power structure inside a government office is a significant achievement in and of itself, and the Sheriff's public apology and concessions on the right of Blacks to protest are seen as victories. But not everyone shares that view:

> The others considered this a victory. We found it a shallow triumph and continued demonstrating until the end of the week when the march from Selma finally began.
> — James Forman, SNCC. [19]

Later that evening, state troopers arrest more than 100 people, mostly students, for picketing on state property at the Capitol.

Judge Johnson Finally Rules

MONTGOMERY: While the protest at the county courthouse is underway, over at federal court, Judge Johnson finally rules on the *Williams v Wallace* petition for an injunction requiring Alabama to permit a march from Selma to Montgomery. Issued nine days after SCLC's case was first filed, his ruling sharply condemns:

> ... an almost continuous pattern of conduct ... on the part of defendant Sheriff Clark, his deputies, and his auxiliary deputies known as 'possemen' of harassment, intimidation, coercion, threatening conduct, and, sometimes, brutal mistreatment... The attempted march alongside U.S. Highway 80... involved nothing more than a peaceful effort on the part of Negro citizens to exercise a classic constitutional right: that is, the right to assemble peaceably and petition one's government for the redress of grievances. — U.S. District Judge Frank Johnson. [11]

Johnson's order closely follows the plan proposed by SCLC. He orders Governor Wallace and the state of Alabama to both facilitate and protect the march. He also orders the federal government to provide whatever assistance the state requires. His ruling specifies that the march is to start on Sunday, March 21, when an unlimited number of protesters are allowed to march out from Selma on the four-lane portion of Highway 80 — known in Alabama as the "Jefferson Davis Highway" — to the first campsite near the Lowndes County line. From there the route to the second and third camps crosses "Bloody" Lowndes. That portion of US 80 is only two lanes wide, and in many places where it traverses boggy swampland, there are no shoulders. In order not to block traffic, Johnson limits the number of marchers to no more than 300. (It's also easier to guard a small number of marchers from Klan snipers although that is not mentioned in Johnson's order.) Once the march reaches Montgomery County, the highway broadens again to four lanes, so from that point into the city an unlimited number can march.

The first three campsites are to be on land owned by courageous Blacks. They know they are risking severe economic — and possibly violent — retaliation for allowing the marchers to use their property. The fourth campsite will be at the City of St. Jude complex in Montgomery. This is a Roman Catholic institution providing education, health, and social services to Blacks. Dr. King's two oldest children were born there. From St. Jude, the march route will take city streets to Dexter Avenue and the steps leading up to the state Capitol where the Tuskegee marchers had been surrounded on March 10.

March 18–20, Organizing the March

SELMA: On Thursday, Friday, and Saturday, SCLC and local leaders work long into the night preparing for the march. Anticipation runs high in Selma and the Black Belt counties. Freedom Movement supporters from all over America begin flowing into Montgomery and Selma by plane, bus, and car. Some come from as far away as Hawaii. Contingents arrive from voting rights battlegrounds in Florida, Mississippi, Louisiana, Georgia, Tennessee, Arkansas, the Carolinas, Virginia and Maryland. They bring with them memories of their own struggles and suffering, and martyrs like Harry & Harriette Moore, Herbert

The Selma Voting Rights Struggle

Lee, James Chaney, Mickey Schwerner, and Andrew Goodman. They all have to be fed and places found for them to sleep.

> Our house was full of people. They'd sleep in sleeping bags on the living-room floor, in the upstairs hallway, anywhere there was space. It was that way everywhere. You had to stand in line to get into the bathroom. What I remember most about those days just before the march was the large groups of people always out by the church singing freedom songs. They'd go on all through the night. I'd fall asleep listening to them. Nothing like this had ever happened before in America; people from all over had come to join us because we were successful in dramatizing that there were wrongs in the South and the time had come to change them. It was more than the right to vote; it was also the way we had been treated. — Sheyann Webb, age 8. [9]

Approval of the march is not universal. The *Atlanta Constitution* is the largest paper in the South and the leading daily newspaper of the "city too busy to hate." Though its front-page motto is *"Covers Dixie Like the Dew,"* it decides to boycott the march, refusing to write about it at all. Alabama's white power structure is, of course, adamantly opposed. Governor Wallace proclaims, postures, and maneuvers, but in President Johnson he meets his match. All his attempts to prevent or subvert the march fail. The Alabama National Guard is federalized, placed under Pentagon command, and ordered to assist the U.S. Army in protecting the marchers.

Within SNCC, attitudes and reactions vary widely. Forman and others continue to oppose the whole idea of a march to Montgomery, viewing it as a meaningless media extravaganza and the "reverend's show." Some SNCC members are so angry at SCLC they're alienated from anything it promotes, and rather than participate many return to the Mississippi projects they were yanked away from after Bloody Sunday. Stokely Carmichael, Bob Mants and a handful of others decide to use King and the march as an organizing opportunity to break the grip of terror that the KKK holds on "Bloody" Lowndes County. Ivanhoe Donaldson and others, however, pitch in to help organize the march despite ambivalence and misgivings. John Lewis, of course, remains steadfast in his support:

> In many ways, [the march] promised to be as big as the March on Washington. The numbers would be nowhere near that many, of course, but unlike the demonstration in Washington, which was a rally more than an actual march, this was literally going to be a mass movement of people, thousands and thousands of them, walking down a highway, cutting through the heart of the state of Alabama. The next five days were a swirl of activity, much like preparing an army for an assault. Marchers, not just from Selma but from across the nation, were mobilized and organized, route sections and schedules were mapped out, printed up and distributed, tents big enough to sleep people by the hundreds were secured. Food, Security, Communications. There were thousands of details to take care of ... — John Lewis, SNCC. [11]

Hosea Williams of SCLC and Ivanhoe Donaldson of SNCC are placed in charge of march preparations and logistics. The most contentious issue is choosing the 300 who will be permitted to march the two days across Lowndes County. Almost everyone wants to be among the select number allowed to go "all the way" for the march's entire 54-mile distance. Many of the visiting dignitaries and organizational leaders push themselves forward to urge the symbolic importance of their inclusion. The final decision is delegated to Ivanhoe Donaldson and Frank Soracco of SNCC. They reserve 250 of the prized slots for Alabama Blacks who had lined up at courthouses to register, been arrested, or faced troopers, clubs, gas, and horses on Bloody Sunday and the hard days that went before. Most are from Selma and Dallas County. The rest from Perry, Wilcox, and Marengo. No one from Lowndes, however, dares risk it. The remaining 50 spots are apportioned among the outside supporters to include

145

The Selma Voting Rights Struggle

representatives of every faith, organization, and institution as well as unique individuals such as old Nannie Washburn, her blind son, and one-legged Jim Letherer who will make the entire march on crutches.

Close to 100 volunteer MCHR doctors and nurses from around the country respond to the call, arriving in Selma with their canvas first-aid satchels. Dr. Aaron Wells of MCHR is placed on the march planning committee to address health issues — sanitary food and water, portable toilets, medical stations, and emergency treatment of wounded should the march be attacked. A fully-equipped mobile hospital is provided by the International Ladies Garment Workers Union (ILGWU) and local Black funeral parlors loan hearses to act as ambulances if needed. The doctors don't screen the chosen marchers, but they do recommend that some with serious health problems drop out. In most cases, their advice not to march is ignored.

Meanwhile the unsung scut-work of organizing logistic support for a multi- day road march with thousands of participants intensifies. Food — where and by whom will it be obtained and cooked, how will it be kept more or less hot and delivered to the marchers on the road? Clean drinking water. Portable toilets. Jackets and rain gear. Tents for sleeping. Sleeping bags. Garbage and trash pickup. Trucks and transport. Radio and walkie-talkie communications. Portable generators for campsites to provide security lights at night. March marshals. Security teams to guard the sleeping marchers. Press and public relations. And, of course, raising funds to pay for it all, to say nothing of the glamorous task of obtaining receipts, recording expenses, and issuing reimbursements. Everyone pitches in, locals and outsiders alike. Precision and coordination range from haphazard to nonexistent, but enthusiasm and energy are high.

> Where do you get food for three thousand people without buying it? ... Well, you pick up the phone and you call the Packinghouse Workers and you say, "We need food, and the march has already started, and they're

The March to Montgomery

gonna bed down in six hours. We need raisins, we need fresh fruit, we need canned fruit, we need gallons of spaghetti, we need gallons of chili beans. Things that you can just take out of the can and heat." See, people forget that there was no food committee and yet there were two and three thousand people to be fed. If a church is gonna entertain two thousand people, they want three or four months to get ready. Then they set up elaborate committees to prepare the food and to serve the food. Well, you might have come into Selma at that time and somebody might have said, "Hey, you wanna work on the food truck?" "Oh, yeah," and at that point you suddenly became a member of the food committee. ... It wasn't planned, it just happened. — Randolph Blackwell, SCLC. [15]

Meanwhile, voter registration efforts and intermittent demonstrations and arrests continue in Selma, Montgomery, and the rural Black Belt counties. Many of those now participating are northerners waiting for the march to commence on Sunday.

NATION: In the North too, there is controversy. In a nationally syndicated newspaper column on March 18 titled, "Danger From the Left," pundits Rowland Evans and Robert Novak label both John Lewis and James Forman, *"two hotheaded extremists,"* who have *"forced"* a *"weak-willed"* Dr. King to resume the Selma march. Using words like, *"capitulated," "abdicated,"* and *"knuckled under,"* they charge King with having surrendered, *"valuable ground to leftist extremists in the drive for control of the civil rights movement."* And, from their Olympian perch they proclaim that SNCC is *"substantially infiltrated by beatnik left-wing revolutionaries, and — worst of all — by Communists."*

Meanwhile, undeterred by these fulminations, hundreds of SNCC-led students continue their sidewalk sit-in on Pennsylvania Avenue in front of the White House, day after day in the snow and rain.

The Selma Voting Rights Struggle

SELMA: On Saturday afternoon, olive-drab jeeps and trucks with a thousand American soldiers appear on city streets as they roll through town to the armory. Soon Army GIs from Fort Bragg in North Carolina and Fort Hood in Texas — white and Black — are standing sentry on street corners, their rifles equipped with fixed bayonets. (They don't know it, but they will soon be on their way to Vietnam, a place they've never heard of.) They are followed by 2,500 sullen members of the now-federalized Alabama National Guard — all white, of course — who resentfully report to their military commanders. Their uniform emblem is the Confederate battle flag, the same flag that flies over the Capitol dome in Montgomery, the same flag that the KKK and white hoodlums wave in opposition to the Freedom Movement. Some of them don't have to travel far, they live in Selma, Montgomery, and adjacent counties. Local Blacks identify among their number some of the possemen who have been beating and lashing protesters.

March 21–24, Marching to Montgomery

BIRMINGHAM: For reasons that are self-evident, Birmingham's nickname is "Bombingham." On Sunday the 21st, the first day of the March to Montgomery, five time-bombs using more than 200 sticks of dynamite are discovered before they explode. One is set to blast through Our Lady of the Universe Catholic Church during Sunday mass. A portable altar is quickly moved outside and the service completed in the parking lot. Another bomb is placed at First Congregational Church where many members of the Black elite worship. A Black high school, the home of Black civil-rights attorney Arthur Shores, and the former home of Dr. King's brother A.D. King are also targeted. Army demolition experts are called in to disarm them.

NATION: Also on Sunday, sympathy marches are held in numerous northern cities including the Bronx where a line of marchers parade down the Grand Concourse to the county courthouse.

The March to Montgomery

SELMA: The March to Montgomery is scheduled to start from Brown Chapel at 10am on Sunday morning. By 11 am, Dr. King and most of the dignitaries have finally arrived to commence the pre-march mass meeting. Well after noon, more than 3,000 marchers begin lining up on Sylvan Street, six-abreast. Just before 1 pm, they step off toward the Edmund Pettus Bridge, which is named for a Confederate general and Grand Dragon of the KKK.

At the head of the line are two American flags and the flag of the United Nations. March leaders and luminaries such as Dr. King, Rabbi Abraham Heschel, UN leader Ralph Bunche, Episcopal Bishop Richard Millard, and others, wear colorful flower leis distributed by the Hawaiian contingent. In the front ranks are Cager Lee (grandfather of Jimmy Lee Jackson), DCVL President F.D. Reese, Dr. King, and SNCC Chairman John Lewis. Holding true to SNCC's position opposing the march, Silas Norman, SNCC's Selma project director, is busy painting the office floor as the singing marchers stream by beneath the windows.

The bulk of the marchers are Black, mostly from Selma and Alabama's Black Belt counties. Also present are representatives from other centers of struggle and resistance across the South, and whites and Blacks from the North and West. As they crest the bridge, they see ahead of them an open highway — no troopers or posse blocking the way.

> This was coming about — this right to be free from fear — in Selma, and it was coming about because of the courage of poor, ordinary black people who knew the time was here. ... What I remember so much about that day was the happiness of the people. I had never seen them like that before. When we finished singing, "We Shall Overcome," we started off and went to the bridge and there were soldiers with rifles and bayonets everywhere, protecting us. Well, when we crossed that bridge and started on down the road for Montgomery, the people just seemed like something had been lifted

The Selma Voting Rights Struggle

from their shoulders. They were so proud, but it was a pride that was dignified. We had always maintained that dignity. — Sheyann Webb. [9]

Escorted by the United States Army and guarded by two helicopters above, the marchers stride past throngs of white hecklers who jeer, curse, and wave Confederate battle flags. Held in check by armed soldiers with bared bayonets, their rage is impotent and futile. The singing marchers ignore them and continue on down US 80 toward Montgomery.

Cruising along the march route are cars with "I hate niggers" and "Yankee trash go home" painted on their sides. The vitriolic hate and obscene verbal violence screamed at the marchers shocks some of the northerners, as do the "news" stories in local papers claiming that the nuns and white women are only there for sexual orgies with Black men. Movement activists who have experienced this form of southern gentility year after year, in state after state, are not perturbed.

HIGHWAY 80: The initial leg of the 54-mile march is short, only seven miles to the first campsite. But seven miles is a long trek for people who usually walk no farther than from a parking lot to a workplace or store. Feet are blistered and legs are sore by the time they reach the David Hall farm where the advance team is raising four large tents for the night's rest. A group led by Professor Elwyn Smith of Pittsburgh Theologic Seminary delivers food to the hungry marchers in a rented truck. Cooked by Black women laboring 16 hours a day in the kitchen at Green Street Baptist Church, the spaghetti, pork & beans, and coffee are ladled out to the marchers from newly-purchased, galvanized steel garbage cans, while squares of corn bread are cut from large baking pans.

Thousands of marchers have to be taken back to Selma, leaving only those permitted on the next two stages through Lowndes County. With night now fallen, and crowds of hostile whites still congregating along the road near the bridge, it's too dangerous to ferry them back to Selma by car. Some are taken by buses using a roundabout route to avoid attack. The remainder are driven to

The March to Montgomery

a nearby railroad stop where a special, nine-car train chartered by the Justice Department returns them to town. Meanwhile, the logistical juggling act continues to produce miracles of improvisation.

> **ATLANTA:** The great fear that Hosea was expressing at that point was that here are all these people pouring in here and we don't have any blankets and we don't have any so-and-so. I remember on one occasion where he was screaming on the phone that he had to have $10,000 for some blankets, and I said, "Hosea, if you just wait, we'll get some blankets." And then we started calling private hospitals and asking if they had blankets in their warehouses that they could lend to us. And somebody in some private hospital, and I don't remember who now, contacted a private hospital in Boston that had closed. And they had something like two thousand blankets. It was a question of how do ya get two thousand blankets out of Boston and into Selma in the space of three hours, because the march was approaching the point where it was to bed down for the first night. Somebody in Boston volunteered a plane, and the blankets were loaded on that plane and flown to Atlanta. I had been soliciting blankets by radio in Atlanta, and we took a truckload of blankets out to the airport. The man opened the back end of the plane, and the plane was stuffed to the brim. We packed those that we had into the plane and the plane flew them into Selma. ... and they were there in time for the first bedding down. We did not have those blankets four hours before they bedded down. — Randolph Blackwell, SCLC. [15]

HIGHWAY 80: The night turns chill as the remaining marchers and support staff wearily fall asleep in separate men's and women's tents (the third tent is for food, supplies, and equipment, and the fourth is the MCHR first aid station). The Alabama National Guard — the "Dixie Division" — is supposed to guard the camp from raiders, but most of them face inward, their

The Selma Voting Rights Struggle

loaded rifles ready to protect the "southern way of life" from the marchers. No one trusts them, so two teams of unarmed Freedom Movement veterans patrol inner and outer perimeters all night, warily watching the guardsmen as carefully as they keep lookout for Klan snipers.

By 6 am the next morning, the temperature has fallen to 28 degrees. Sparkling white frost crusts the leaves, and water buckets have a thin skin of ice. The marchers wake stiff and cold from sleeping on hard ground. *The New York Times* reports that, *"At dawn the encampment resembled a cross between a 'Grapes of Wrath' migrant labor camp and the Continental Army bivouac at Valley Forge. The marchers, bundled to the ears with blankets and quilts huddled around the fires..."* Since long before sunrise, the women in the Green Street kitchen have been cooking breakfast of oatmeal, toast, and coffee, which is trucked to the campsite and ladled out from the same metal trash cans used the night before (carefully cleaned under MCHR supervision, of course).

By 7 am, the 300 officially permitted marchers are on the road for the 16-mile leg to the second campsite. More bombs have been found and disarmed in Birmingham, and Army demolition experts carefully inspect each bridge as the marchers move east.

For those living by the side of the road, the first sign of the march is the loud, "Thwop-thwop-thwop" of helicopters circling above. A state trooper car appears on the road with its warning lights flashing. It moves slowly at footstep pace. It's followed by Army jeeps containing rifle-armed soldiers. Then come the lead marchers with an American flag waving in the wind, and behind them are the marching 300 — men and women, mostly Black but with a portion of whites too, some old, some young, some in the prime of life. They are singing, and talking, and walking proud. Behind them come the vans and cars of the news media, their cameras clicking and whirring. Then come the medical van and trucks carrying portable toilets, and finally more soldiers and trooper cars.

The March to Montgomery

With laughter and derisive comments, the marchers pass White Citizens Council billboards that inaccurately claim to show "Martin Luther King at a Communist Training School." (The photo had been shot during an address he gave at the Highlander Folk School). The sun turns bright on the open stretches and sunburn becomes a problem. MCHR nurses distribute white sunscreen lotion, which some young marchers use to write "Vote" on their foreheads.

LOWNDES COUNTY: They're in Lowndes County now, mostly pastures and occasional cotton or cornfield alternating with stretches of swamp where gloomy trees trail long veils of Spanish moss and the dark water is slimy with algae. Charles Fager of SCLC recalls: *"The [dead] trees seemed like the stumps of burned crosses, and it was easy to imagine mutilated black bodies, the victims of [the] county's quiet methods of social control, bloated and rising suddenly out of the mud ..."*

The population of Lowndes is 81% Black and the county is ruled by white-terror. The story of "Bloody" Lowndes is a tale of racially motivated land seizures, murders, evictions, exploitation, beatings, arson, and frame-ups on false charges. Like other Black Belt counties, there's a secret thread of covert resistance to white supremacy that runs hidden beneath the surface. At first, the few isolated Blacks living in dilapidated, "shotgun shacks" along the highway watch the march go by in silent astonishment. No one in Lowndes has ever seen such a public display of Black pride, Black assertiveness, and Black opposition to discrimination, racism, and white power. Equally astounding is the sight of Black and white men and women, marching together as friends and allies. As word spreads through the grapevine, Blacks begin gathering along the road.

At Trickem crossroads, a score or more Blacks are waiting when the march arrives. Though they know they are under observation by hostile whites, they move onto the highway to welcome the Freedom marchers with smiles and waves and cheers. Juanita Huggins raises her strong voice in, *"Lord, I Cannot Stay on This Highway by Myself."* Dr. King and others join her.

The Selma Voting Rights Struggle

> After lunch the march passed through Trickem, which was not a town at all but just an intersection with a name. A small, dilapidated black Baptist church stood at the crossroads, and not far from it a rundown white building with a rusty tin roof that looked abandoned and thus went unnoticed by the leaders in the front line. But this building, with holes in the wall, cardboard over the missing panes of window glass and whole sections of the tin roof gone exposing the beams, was not abandoned; it was the Rolen school, one of almost a score of similar rundown structures the county maintained after its fashion for the 80 per cent black majority of its citizens. Inside it three teachers tried to teach two grades each in the three rooms, and during the winter the students had to wear their coats and boots in class because the wind came right through the walls. The latrine was out in back. — Charles Fager, SCLC. [10]

Later on, Napoleon Mays, deacon of Mt. Gillard church joins the march with his children, nieces, and nephews. Further down the road so does old Frank Haralson who with the aid of his cane, limps the last miles to the second campsite. The hidden thread of Black resistance in Lowndes County that began emerging into public view when John Hulett led 37 courageous souls to register at the Hayneville courthouse back in February is stronger now and rising to the surface. One march participant recalls the response of Blacks to the march:

> If you look at the photos of the people who are watching the march, there was such joy on their faces, such an emotional feeling, and that was true for the whole march all the way through, Selma — Lowndes — Montgomery. [16]

The second campsite is infested with swarms of red ants that bedevil the marchers whenever they sit to eat or lie down to sleep. It is on land owned by Mrs. Rosie Steele, a Black woman 78 years old:

The March to Montgomery

At first I didn't think it amounted to much, I guess I've lived too long and just didn't think things would change — until I heard the president's speech the other night. ... When they come to me and asked me if they could use my land I felt I couldn't afford to turn them down. If the president can take a stand, I guess I can too. ... I don't know, I almost feel like I might live long enough to vote myself. — Mrs. Rosie Steele. [10]

Selma is now more than 20 miles distant, and when the trashcans of spaghetti finally arrive, the food is cold and congealing. Black women in Lowndes County send as much food as they can to supplement the marcher's meager rations. That night it begins to rain. By mid-morning, a light drizzle becomes a heavy downpour. The marchers hit the road early after lukewarm coffee and a breakfast gone cold. They try to remain dry with make-do ponchos made from plastic garbage bags and improvised hats from flattened corn-flake boxes, but the wind blows hard and spray is kicked up by passing cars. Soon they're drenched to the bone. Loaded on a stake-bed truck, their bedrolls are soaked through. Someone starts a chant of *"Freedom! Free-Dom! Free-Dom!"* In driving rain they cross over Big Swamp on a long causeway raised above the black water. *"Free-Dom! Free-Dom! Free- Dom!"*

John Doar of the Justice Department manages to get an order sent down through the Pentagon bureaucracy commanding the Dixie Division to face outward to protect the marchers from Lowndes County rather than vice versa. Sullenly, resentfully, they comply.

For some marchers, cheap, fake-leather shoes are all they own and now they're falling apart. One young woman tapes cellophane around her feet to keep on marching. Legs and feet are sore, soaking wet garments chafe and rub, blisters ache and burn with every step. *"Free-Dom! Free-Dom! Free-Dom!"*

The third campsite is on the Robert Gardener farm, owned by A.G. Gaston of Birmingham. Though the rain has now dwindled to an intermittent drizzle, the site is soggy and dotted with puddles. The dark soil has turned to thick, sticky mud that oozes over shoes and glues down feet. Unless you step carefully, your shoe remains stuck and your sock-clad foot plops down into the wet slimy goo. The advance crew spreads hay on the ground, but that just thickens the quagmire. Tuskegee students provide dinner of BBQ chicken, hash, peas, and carrots. It has to be eaten either standing on tired feet or sitting in the mud. Cheap air mattresses have been obtained from somewhere and people try to sleep on them, but many deflate in the night and marchers awake in the cold ooze.

Breakfast the next morning is cold coffee, cold toast, and cold oatmeal. Almost no one has managed to have a good night's sleep. Everyone is caked with mud, sullen, and gritty-eyed. But the day dawns warm, and as they hit the road, a song soars up into a bright blue sky. The marchers begin shedding their jackets and ponchos, piling them into the supply truck. Then they are abruptly soaked by a sudden spring shower.

They cross into Montgomery County, and the highway again widens to four lanes. Busses, cars, and pickup trucks ferry in marchers from Selma and Montgomery. The passengers jump out and join the line that steadily grows from 300 to 500, from 500 to a 1,000. As the march passes through the Montgomery outskirts, it swells to 2,500. And, it's 5,000 strong when it finally swings through the gates of St. Jude where thousands more are waiting to greet them.

MONTGOMERY: Some 200 Tuskegee, Alabama State, and Montgomery high school students, just released on bond after days in Kilby prison and other lockups, proudly march into St. Jude to join the swelling throng. And, "like a tide coming in, inevitable and relentless," a steady flow of Movement supporters from South and North arrive for the final leg of the march to the state Capitol. As the numbers pass 10,000 and exhaustion overcomes the work crews, logistic support falters. An old generator fails, plunging portions of the campground into periods of partial darkness. The food truck can't get through the crush or find the 300 road-marchers to deliver dinner. Poles for two of the field tents break and they partly collapse. Trucks and vehicles become mired in the mud, which is almost as thick and gooey as the previous campsite on the Gardener farm.

That night, luminaries of stage and screen mobilized by Harry Belafonte put on a free "Stars for Freedom" performance for the huge crowd. From an improvised outdoor stage laid atop coffins loaned by Black funeral homes, Mahalia Jackson, Dick Gregory, Joan Baez, Leonard Bernstein, Nina Simone, Nipsey Russel, Peter, Paul and Mary, Pete Seeger, Sammy Davis, Odetta, Ossie Davis, Ruby Dee, Ella Fitzgerald, and scores of others, greet and entertain the throng. Though, as one marcher later recalls:

> We arrived at St. Jude, which is this kind of big school, I think, or a hospital or something, and they had this entertainment show, with all these movie stars. I was so exhausted that as I stumbled into the tent, I could hear Peter, Paul and Mary start to sing something somewhere in the distance. That was the last thing I knew until the next morning, when somebody kicked me awake. I missed the whole thing. [16]

March 25, Marching on the Capitol

MONTGOMERY: Light, intermittent rain drifts down as thousands of marchers gather on Thursday morning for the final push through Montgomery to the state Capitol. Security is tight, so tight that Army sentries won't let the car carrying Dr. King enter the St. Jude gate. Andrew Young, then Ralph Bunch of the United Nations, and finally King himself try to talk their way past the young sergeant dutifully manning his post. To no avail. Finally, a Montgomery motorcycle cop recognizes King and tells the GI, *"You danged fool. This is the man! Let him through!"*

There is confusion too on the grounds of St. Jude. The plan is for King and the 300 to lead the march to the Capitol. Ivanhoe Donaldson and Frank Soracco hand out orange highway-safety vests to identify them, but many others demand the honor of wearing the vests and leading the march. Some of the out-of-

The Selma Voting Rights Struggle

town preachers and organization leaders insist they are entitled to march side by side with King and they resent having to follow behind "kids." The young stalwarts who marched all the way will have none of that. Selma student Profit Barlow (17) shouts back, *"All you dignitaries got to get behind me. I didn't see any of you fellows in Selma, and I didn't see you on the way to Montgomery. Ain't nobody going to get in front of me but Dr. King!"*

Before King can join the line of marchers, Montgomery County sheriff's deputies serve him and other Movement leaders with multiple lawsuits and summonses for a variety of offenses and claims, all of which they will have to answer in court over the days to come. As King tries to take his place at the head of the march, a surge of the self-important, eager to be seen and photographed next to him, overwhelm the marshals. Rosa Parks is rudely shoved aside. She finds a place farther back among the rank and file. SCLC's field staff place the 300 in their orange vests ahead of King as an honor vanguard, leaving behind them an open space for reporters to photograph the march "leaders" (both invited and self-appointed).

The march finally gets underway almost two hours behind schedule — not that unusual for freedom marches. Singing strong, more than 12,000 stride out of St. Jude's. An even greater number are waiting to join the line at various staging areas along the four-mile route to the Capitol.

As it flows through the city — growing larger block by block — the march passes Holt Street Baptist Church where in 1955 a very young Dr. King had addressed the first mass meeting of the Montgomery Bus Boycott. Then it passes near the Greyhound Bus station where the Freedom Riders were so brutally beaten in 1961. As Rosa Parks turns up Dexter Avenue, she passes the bus stop where on a dank, dreary night less than ten years ago, she had refused to move to the back of the bus and endured the humiliation and terror of a lonely arrest. Today she is no longer alone. Today she proudly walks with 25,000 other freedom fighters — Black and white.

The March to Montgomery

When the march enters the downtown business district, the streets are eerily quiet. Governor Wallace has urged whites to stay away and has proclaimed a "danger holiday" for female employees (whites only, of course). Lines of troopers guard every foot of state property. Plywood has been placed over the bronze plaque on the marble plaza to prevent any Black feet from "desecrating" the spot where Jefferson Davis was sworn in as President of the Confederate States of America in 1861.

The march line is so long, it takes over an hour for all of the marchers to finally arrive and fill the full, 8-lane width of Dexter Avenue from the foot of the Capitol steps back for blocks. Law enforcement authorities — no friends of the Freedom Movement — place the total number of marchers at 25,000. The media, and later historians to this day, accept and repeat that figure without question. Movement organizers and participants estimate the number to be much higher, but there is no consensus as to the total. In the final analysis though, what defines this march is not total numbers, but rather *who* the marchers are — most of them are hard-working southern Blacks — maids, sharecroppers, laborers, farmers, and a smattering of teachers and business owners — all determined to end white supremacy and its "southern way of life." Though the overwhelming majority of the marchers are Black and poor, the media focus, as usual, is on the white and notable.

The speakers' platform is a flatbed truck equipped with microphones and loudspeakers. The rally begins with songs by Odetta, Oscar Brand, Joan Baez, Len Chandler, Peter, Paul & Mary, and Leon Bibb. The event is broadcast live on national TV, but when Mary Travers — blond and beautiful — joyfully kisses Harry Belafonte on the cheek, so many outraged whites swamp studio phone lines that CBS switches to their regular soap operas until a flood of equally angry viewers on the other side force them to restore coverage.

Dr. King delivers the main address, which today is known as the, *"Our God is Marching On,"* speech. He begins by outlining the long history of racism and discrimination faced by Blacks

The Selma Voting Rights Struggle

in Alabama, the South, and America, and he pays tribute to the equally long history of Black resistance to white supremacy from Montgomery to Birmingham to Selma and back again to this day in Montgomery. Then he lays it on the line, calling out and describing the economic foundations of segregation.

> "The segregation of the races was really a political stratagem employed by the emerging Bourbon interests in the South to keep the southern masses divided and southern labor the cheapest in the land. You see, it was a simple thing to keep the poor white masses working for near-starvation wages in the years that followed the Civil War. Why, if the poor white plantation or mill worker became dissatisfied with his low wages, the plantation or mill owner would merely threaten to fire him and hire former Negro slaves and pay him even less. Thus, the southern wage level was kept almost unbearably low."

(The term, "Bourbon" as used in this context by Dr. King, refers to the very wealthy and very white southern elite — government leaders, plantation owners, mining, and manufacturing kingpins, major bank financiers, and large cotton merchants. Economically and politically, this group dominated the South before the Civil War and quickly regained their power after Reconstruction.)

> "Toward the end of the Reconstruction era, something very significant happened. That is what was known as the Populist Movement. The leaders of this movement began awakening the poor white masses and the former Negro slaves to the fact that they were being fleeced by the emerging Bourbon interests. Not only that, but they began uniting the Negro and white masses into a voting bloc that threatened to drive the Bourbon interests from the command posts of political power in the South.
>
> "To meet this threat, the southern aristocracy began immediately to engineer this development of a segregated

The March to Montgomery

society. I want you to follow me through here because this is very important to see the roots of racism and the denial of the right to vote. Through their control of mass media, they revised the doctrine of white supremacy. They saturated the thinking of the poor white masses with it, thus clouding their minds to the real issue involved in the Populist Movement. They then directed the placement on the books of the South of laws that made it a crime for Negroes and whites to come together as equals at any level. And that did it. That crippled and eventually destroyed the Populist Movement of the nineteenth century. If it may be said of the slavery era that the white man took the world and gave the Negro Jesus, then it may be said of the Reconstruction era that the southern aristocracy took the world and gave the poor white man Jim Crow."

King honors the people of Selma and all others who have fought, and struggled, and sometimes died for freedom. He declares that racism and violence will not stop the Freedom Movement which will keep on marching:

"Let us therefore continue our triumphant march to the realization of the American dream. Let us march on segregated housing until every ghetto or social and economic depression dissolves, and Negroes and whites live side by side in decent, safe, and sanitary housing. Let us march on segregated schools until every vestige of segregated and inferior education becomes a thing of the past, and Negroes and whites study side-by-side in the socially-healing context of the classroom. Let us march on poverty until no American parent has to skip a meal so that their children may eat. Let us march until no starved man walks the streets of our cities and towns in search of jobs that do not exist. Let us march on poverty until wrinkled stomachs in Mississippi are filled, and the idle industries of Appalachia are realized and revitalized,

The Selma Voting Rights Struggle

and broken lives in sweltering ghettos are mended and remolded."

After exposing the fallacy of a "normalcy" that is a normalcy of poverty, injustice, violence, and murder he declares that:

"The only normalcy that we will settle for is the normalcy that allows justice to run down like waters, and righteousness like a mighty stream. The only normalcy that we will settle for is the normalcy of brotherhood, the normalcy of true peace, the normalcy of justice.

From his truck-bed podium, King can clearly see Dexter Avenue Baptist Church where 10 years earlier he began his ministry and rose to leadership of the Montgomery Bus Boycott. Perhaps that personal journey is in his thoughts as he proclaims a declaration of faith that still rings across time:

"I know you are asking today, "How long will it take?" ... Somebody's asking, "When will wounded justice, lying prostrate on the streets of Selma and Birmingham and communities all over the South, be lifted from this dust of shame to reign supreme among the children of men?" ... I come to say to you this afternoon, however difficult the moment, however frustrating the hour, it will not be long, because "truth crushed to earth will rise again."

"How long? Not long, because "No lie can live forever."

How long? Not long, because "You shall reap what you sow."

How long? Not long:

Truth forever on the scaffold,

Wrong forever on the throne,

The March to Montgomery

Yet that scaffold sways the future,

And, behind the dim unknown,

Standeth God within the shadow,

Keeping watch above his own.

How long? Not long, because the arc of the moral universe is long, but it bends toward justice.

How long? Not long, because:

Mine eyes have seen the glory of the coming of the Lord;

He is trampling out the vintage where the grapes of wrath are stored;

He has loosed the fateful lightning of his terrible swift sword;

His truth is marching on.

He has sounded forth the trumpet that shall never call retreat;

He is sifting out the hearts of men before His judgment seat.

O, be swift, my soul, to answer Him! Be jubilant my feet!

Our God is marching on.

Glory, hallelujah! Glory, hallelujah!

Glory, hallelujah! Glory, hallelujah!

His truth is marching on."

chapter 4

Aftermath

For many participants, the Selma Voting Rights Campaign, the March to Montgomery, and the rally at the Alabama Capitol steps are the political and emotional peak of the Freedom Movement — its greatest and most shining moment. And for some, the campaign and march are the high point of nonviolence as a strategy of social change. Though he remains steadfast in his nonviolent commitment, John Lewis notes:

> We're only flesh. I could understand people not wanting to get beaten anymore. The body gets tired. You put out so much energy and you saw such little gain. Black capacity to believe white would really open his heart, open his life to nonviolent appeal, was running out. — John Lewis. [11]

The struggle for the vote neither began nor ended in Selma. Rather it was built on a foundation going back decades and it was pushed forward in the early 1960s by hard and dangerous campaigns throughout the South. But it is the battle for the vote in the Alabama Black Belt — based on, and building from, all that came before — that finally forces passage of the Voting Rights Act of 1965, perhaps the most politically significant victory of the entire Civil Rights Movement.

Yet despite eventual passage of the Voting Rights Act in August of 1965, white segregationists continue to use violence and economic retaliation to deny nonwhites any share of democratic political power. Their efforts include attempting to keep Blacks from registering, preventing the new voters from exercising their rights

The Selma Voting Rights Struggle

or running for office, and blocking the election of candidates who are independent of the white power structure. Throughout the Deep South as the Freedom Movement struggles on in the months and years that follow the Montgomery March, more Freedom Movement activists are assassinated, more churches and homes are bombed, more protests are suppressed with police clubs, tear-gas, and mass arrests. More Blacks are thrown off their land and evicted from their homes, and more Afro-Americans are fired from their jobs.

In the summer of 1965, northern volunteers again come South to put their bodies on the line in support of southern Blacks fighting to be free. In 1966, the Meredith March Against Fear pushes its way through half of Mississippi. A freedom march to Baton Rouge occurs in Louisiana while other states experience mass protests too. Though scarcely reported by the national media, local organizing and protests in many communities continue into the 1970s.

Though federal enforcement of the Voting Rights Act is initially reluctant and half-hearted, gradually it begins to take effect and the number of Black voters increases significantly. In towns and counties with Black voting majorities, by the late 1960s and early 1970s, Black candidates are elected to office. In places where Black voters remain a minority, white elected officials come to realize that they have to recognize, and to some degree serve Blacks as well as whites. Bribery and rigged elections remain common, though, as do efforts to control and constrain Black political power.

For Alabama Blacks, perhaps even more important than the Voting Rights Act is the sense of human dignity and self-respect they win through their own courage, determination, and endurance. They stand against — and overcome — the forces of violent segregation and state power that for so many generations have dominated their lives. This is something they achieve themselves; it's not the work of lawyers in distant courts, nor lobbyists nor legislators in the halls of power. They know, of course, that racism, poverty, economic injustice, and exploitation

Aftermath

are not ended, but they also know they've struck a blow from which the old system of ruthlessly enforced social and political subservience can never recover. In a very real and personal sense, they understand that though its death throes might linger for years, the *southern way of life* died on the Edmund Pettus bridge, March 7, 1965 — killed by the raw courage and determination of ordinary Black folk, maids and day laborers, farmers and teachers, and above all, heroic young students.

> As I look back on it, I think the real victory wasn't the fact that we went to Montgomery and had that rally. The real victory was just winning the right to do that. That fifty-mile march was symbolic. The real triumph had been on March the 7th at the bridge and at the church afterwards, when we turned a brutal beating into a nonviolent victory.—Sheyann Webb. [9]

Murder and Character Assassination of Viola Liuzzo

It's late afternoon when the marchers begin to disperse after the freedom rally at the Alabama Capitol. From the moment they leave Brown Chapel in Selma to the end of the program in Montgomery, the U.S. Army and federal law enforcement agencies keep everyone safe — no one has been seriously injured. But now, the elaborate protection system begins to wind down just as tens of thousands of people head home. Unfamiliar with Montgomery streets, thousands of northern supporters, who came directly to the city, need help finding the homes and churches where their luggage is waiting and then transportation to airports and bus depots. Since passage of the Civil Rights Act, Black-owned taxis are now legally permitted to carry white passengers, but they are overwhelmed and white taxis want nothing to do with "agitators" and "race-mixers." Thousands of Blacks need to return to Selma, and thousands more to Wilcox, Perry, and other Alabama counties and communities. What little

The Selma Voting Rights Struggle

money SCLC has left is used to charter some buses, but most people have to be ferried back along US 80 in hastily organized carpools.

Mrs. Viola Liuzzo, wife of a Teamsters Union organizer, grew up poor and white in Georgia, yet she refused to adopt the racist attitudes held by many of her friends and neighbors. At the age of 17, she migrated to Detroit where she found work in the booming war industries. There she lived, and married, and had five daughters and sons. Among her friends are both Black and white. A member of both the NAACP and the Unitarian church, she has long been active in Detroit civil rights campaigns. On March 16, she answers Dr. King's call. Driving alone in her big Oldsmobile, it takes her three days to reach Selma where she volunteers with different work teams including the transportation committee. She marches over the bridge on the first day of the five-day march and marches from St. Jude's to the Capitol on the last day.

Leroy Moton, tall and thin, is a 19-year-old Black voting rights activist from Selma. He too is on the transportation committee. When the Montgomery rally ends, the two of them fill Mrs. Liuzzo's car with marchers and ferry them to Selma. Then they head back toward Montgomery to pick up another load.

By now, it's dusk. Loitering in Selma's Silver Moon Cafe is a Klan "action team" of four KKK members from Bessemer, a suburb of Birmingham. The four are William Eaton, Eugene Thomas, Collie Wilkins, and Gary Rowe. They're hard-core Klansmen, well experienced in violence and brutality. Though the first three don't know it, Rowe is also a paid informant for the FBI and has been so for many years. All day they've been in Eugene's Chevy Impala trying to get close enough to kill Dr. King, but Army security has been too tight. As night falls, they are disappointed and discouraged

Elmer Cook, one of the three men who killed Rev. Reeb stops by their table. "*I did my job,*" he says, "*now you go and do yours.*" They return to their car and go hunting for someone to kill. On Broad Street, they spot an Oldsmobile with Michigan plates

Aftermath

heading for the bridge. A white woman is driving. Her passenger is a Black man. They have their target. The four Klansmen follow her over the bridge, hanging back until they clear the state troopers and Army jeeps still patrolling the four-lane segment of Highway 80 leading out of Selma.

Out on the dark, two-lane stretch of US 80 in Lowndes County, Liuzzo and Moton suddenly realize they are being chased. She floors it, hoping to outrun their pursuers. The Klan car is faster. Slowly it gains on them. On a long straight section with no oncoming traffic, Thomas manages to draw up alongside. The other three open fire with pistols. Mrs. Liuzzo is shot through the head, killing her instantly. She slumps over, her foot no longer on the gas. The attackers surge ahead. The Oldsmobile swerves off the road into the shoulder ditch and then up the slope of a small embankment. Moton, unwounded but covered in Viola's blood, grabs the steering wheel and manages to bring the careening car to a stop.

The Klansmen turn around and come back. They shine a light though the shattered window glass. Moton feigns death. The Klansmen drive off. Moton flags down a truck carrying marchers home from Montgomery. They take him back to Selma. The cops arrest him.

News of Mrs. Liuzzo's murder is flashed to Washington. FBI Director Hoover informs President Johnson and Attorney General Katzenbach that an informer was in the Klan car. Though he has not yet received any report from Rowe, he assures them that his unnamed operative had no gun and did no shooting — which he later learns is not the case. Hoover echoes segregationist slanders and slurs, falsely accusing Mrs. Liuzzo of having needle marks on her arm from taking drugs, and "necking" with Moton who, he claims, was *"snuggling up close to the white woman."*

What he does not reveal to the President (or anyone outside the Bureau) is that Rowe's FBI handlers had known in advance, and granted permission, for him to ride with the KKK "action team" that intended to kill Dr. King. And the Bureau made no effort to place them under surveillance or prevent them from committing murder.

Nor does Hoover reveal that for the past five years while working as a paid FBI informant, Rowe has simultaneously been an active and aggressive Klansman. The Bureau knows that he shot a Black man in the chest during turmoil over school integration and, though never charged, he was suspected of complicity in the Birmingham Church bombing that killed four little girls. They also know that he participated in the savage mob attack on the Freedom Riders in Birmingham. Rowe had warned the FBI in advance that the beating was going to take place — but the FBI did nothing to prevent it. Neither did they use Rowe's information to arrest the perpetrators. Nor did they ever act on any of the other racial crimes he participated in and reported to them.

All of this is kept hidden until 1975, three years after Hoover's death. Idaho Senator Frank Church leads investigations by the Senate Select Committee to Study Governmental Operations with Regard to Intelligence Activities (Church Committee) that publicly reveal the concealed story of the FBI's relation with Rowe. A history that is then confirmed by a special Justice Department investigation report titled, *The FBI, the Department of Justice, and Gary Thomas Rowe.*

On Friday afternoon, less than 24 hours after Liuzzo's death, Johnson, Hoover, and Katzenbach announce the arrest of the four Klansmen. Charges against Rowe are dropped and he is given immunity in return for testifying against the other three. Murder is a state crime, and Alabama immediately releases the killers on bail. Segregationist whites now add "Open Season" bumper stickers to accompany their Confederate-flag license plates. Other than the assassins themselves, Leroy Moton is the only eyewitness to the murder. When he is released from jail, he is sent north for safety so the Klan can't murder him before he testifies.

On May 3rd, six weeks after the murder, Collie Wilkins is put on trial. Whites jam the Lowndes County courthouse in Hayneville to show their support for a KKK killer. Blacks dare not attend.

Aftermath

The jury, of course, is all white. In accordance with southern tradition, the jury is also all male (white women being considered too pure, fragile, and delicate, to face the brutal underpinnings of the southern way of life).

The prosecution presents an irrefutable case of first degree (premeditated) murder, laying out both forensic and investigative evidence, and the eyewitness testimony of both Leroy Moton and Gary Rowe, who is now revealed under heavy guard as an FBI informant. During cross examination, Matt Murphy, the Klan's lawyer (or "Klonsel"), accuses Moton of shooting Liuzzo after having "interracial sex" with her, *under the hypnotic spell of narcotics.*" Robert Shelton, Imperial Wizard of the Alabama KKK, sits with Wilkins at the defendant's table. After the prosecution rests its case, Murphy offers a cursory 20-minute defense. Then he attacks the prosecution and the victim. He characterizes Mrs. Liuzzo as, "*A white nigger who turned her car over to a black nigger for the purpose of hauling niggers and communists back and forth.*"

 He accuses Rowe of being a liar, "*... as treacherous as a rattlesnake ... a traitor and a pimp and an agent of Castro and I don't know what all,*" for violating his Klan oath of loyalty and secrecy.

Though Wilkin's guilt is obvious, reporters and white onlookers assume the local white jury will quickly acquit him — as is the southern custom in racial cases. To everyone's surprise, the jury fails to bring back a swift verdict of innocent on all counts. Instead, their deliberations are carried over to the next day. A mistrial is declared when the jury reports they are hopelessly deadlocked 10-2 for conviction on a manslaughter charge. This means they've chosen not to reach a guilty verdict on first- or second-degree murder, but 10 of them are willing to convict on the lesser charge of manslaughter (killing in the heat of understandable passion without premeditation or malice aforethought).

Some reporters believe that 10 Lowndes County whites willing to

The Selma Voting Rights Struggle

convict a Klansman of *anything* is a sign of racial progress. But most Movement activists assume it's because the victim was both white and a woman. They believe that if it had been Leroy Moton shot in the head, or a white male activist like Mickey Schwerner, a quick verdict of not guilty would have been returned.

Syndicated journalist Inez Robb is the only reporter who dares raise a fundamental question:

> What sorely troubles me, if we accept the prosecution's account of the slaying, is the moral aspect of Rowe's presence in the car ... Under what kind of secret orders did Rowe work? [Was he expected to join in crime, strictly observe, or try to prevent murder?] It is one woman's opinion that the FBI owes the nation an explanation of its action in the Liuzzo case. — Inez Robb. [8]

No explanation is ever forthcoming from the FBI. Bureau Director Hoover's personal vindictiveness against anyone who questions or criticizes either himself or the Bureau is notorious. It is also well known among politicians, publishers, reporters, and others involved in national politics that, for decades, he has carefully built a collection of secret files containing derogatory and damaging information on the power elite. Commonly known as the "Hoover files," most of the information he collects is personal, political, financial, or sexual rather than criminal. Unsavory or embarrassing personal secrets of reporters or publishers who anger the Director are leaked to the media and surreptitiously passed to spouses, employers, colleagues, and competitors. Intimidated by this smear machine, no one in the media follows up on Inez Robb's question.

On October 20, Wilkins is placed on trial a second time. Again, Leroy Moton and Rowe testify. Replacing Murphy as defense counsel is former FBI agent and Birmingham Mayor Arthur Hanes. Like Murphy, he vilifies Mrs. Liuzzo and smears Moton, asking, *"Leroy, was it part of your duties as transportation officer to make love to Mrs. Liuzzo?"*

Aftermath

This time the all-white, all-male, Lowndes County jury requires just 90 minutes to return a verdict of not guilty on all charges.

In December 1965, Collie Wilkins, William Eaton, and Eugene Thomas, are tried by John Doar in federal court before Judge Frank Johnson. They are convicted of violating Mrs. Liuzzo's civil rights and sentenced to the maximum term of 10 years in prison. Rowe is given a $10,000 bonus by the FBI (equal to about $73,000 in 2012). He disappears into the secrecy of witness protection.

Meanwhile, hidden from public view, Hoover and the FBI wage a covert COINTELPRO campaign of character assassination to defame Mrs. Liuzzo. Starting immediately after her murder, a steady stream of lies and innuendoes are leaked to the press, whispered to high government officials, and surreptitiously passed to community and religious leaders. Without a shred of evidence, the Bureau alleges that she was sexually promiscuous, a drug user, a Communist, and an *"outside agitator"* who had *"abandoned her family"* to *"cause trouble in the South"* (Hoover's words). In part, these fantasies no doubt reflect Hoover's personal prejudices, but their main purpose is to deflect attention from the Bureau's long-standing relationship with Rowe, their failure to prevent violence or make arrests in race-related cases, and their legal and moral responsibility for Mrs. Liuzzo's death.

The mid-1970s Justice Department report, "The FBI, the Justice Department, and Gary Thomas Rowe," reveals that during the 1965 trials, Rowe repeatedly lied under oath about his Klan activities. The report concludes that FBI officials knew at the time that he was committing perjury, and that they engaged in an officially sanctioned cover-up to keep the truth hidden.

In 1977, the Liuzzo children manage to obtain her FBI file through the Freedom of Information Act and discover that the Bureau had orchestrated a covert slander and smear campaign to vilify their mother. They file a lawsuit claiming that the FBI knew

The Selma Voting Rights Struggle

Rowe and the other Klansmen were out to kill, and that by failing to take action, the Bureau effectively conspired in her murder. A judge dismisses their case in 1983, ruling there is no evidence of an FBI conspiracy to kill Mrs. Liuzzo *specifically,* and that the FBI could not be held liable for failing to prevent a crime.

When subpoenaed by a grand jury, Wilkins and Thomas testify that it was Rowe who had actually shot Mrs. Liuzzo. They pass a lie-detector test and two Birmingham cops testify that Rowe bragged to them that he was the one who killed her. Rowe is indicted for her murder in 1978, but the federal government quashes the case based on his immunity deal for testifying in the 1965 trials. Without an impartial investigation and trial, it is impossible to determine who is telling the truth — Rowe, a violent Klansman and informer, or the two convicted killers and police witnesses from a department known to be infiltrated by the Ku Klux Klan.

Appendix

Voting Rights and So-Called "Literacy Tests"

Prior to passage of the federal Voting Rights Act in 1965, many southern states maintained elaborate voter registration procedures whose purpose was to prevent nonwhites from voting. This process was generally referred to as the "literacy test." But it was much more than simply a reading test; it was an entire complex system devoted to denying Afro-Americans (and in some regions, Latinos and Native Americans) the right to vote.

The "literacy test" and registration procedures were just part of a larger interlocking system of racial discrimination in regards to voting. The all-white, state, county, and local police forces intimidated and harassed Blacks who tried to register. They arrested would-be voters on false charges and beat others for imagined transgressions. Throughout the Deep South, white businessmen, employers, bank officials, and landlords were organized into White Citizens Councils that inflicted economic retaliation against nonwhites who tried to vote — evictions, firings, boycotts, foreclosures, and loan denials.

When economic pressure proved insufficient, the Ku Klux Klan was ready with violence and mayhem — cross-burnings, night riders, beatings, rapes, church burnings and home bombings. Those who organized and campaigned for access to the ballot faced murder and mob lynchings, drive-by shootings and sniper assassinations. Today the Klan would be labeled "terrorists," but back then, the white establishment saw them as defenders of the "southern way of life" and upholders of "our glorious southern heritage."

The Selma Voting Righs Struggle

Registering to Vote in Alabama

While in theory there were standard statewide registration procedures, in real life, the individual county registrars did things their own way. The exact procedures varied from county to county, and within a county, they varied over time as the registrars devised new tactics to evade compliance with federal court rulings.

If you were an Afro-American living in the Black Belt of Alabama in 1965, a typical registration process looked something like this: You have to go down to the courthouse to register. In the rural counties where most Black folk live, the Registrar's Office is open only every other Monday for a few hours, usually in the morning or afternoon. You have to take off work to register — with or without your employer's permission. If your white employer gives permission, or fails to fire a Black who tries to vote, he risks the White Citizens Council driving him out of business with an economic boycott — customers will be warned off, banks will refuse loans, vendors will not sell supplies, and so on.

On the occasional registration day, the county sheriff and his deputies make it their business to hang around the courthouse to discourage "undesirables" (like you) from trying to register. This means that Black women and men have to run a gauntlet of intimidation, insults, threats, and sometimes arrest on phony charges, just to get to the registration office. Once inside the registrar's office, they face hatred, harassment, and humiliation from clerks and officials.

The Alabama Voter Application Form you have to fill out, and the oaths you have to sign, are four pages long. It is designed to intimidate and threaten. You have to swear that your answers to every single question are true under penalty of perjury. You know the information you enter on the form will be passed on to the Citizens Council and KKK. If you tell the truth, you put

Literacy Tests for Voting Eligibility

yourself, your family, and your friends in danger. If you lie, you risk prison.

After filling out the Application Form you take the "literacy test," which is far more than simply a test of your reading ability — you are asked to read, copy, and interpret to the satisfaction of the registrar a section of the state constitution and then answer obscure questions on government and civics.

Many counties use what they called the "voucher system." This means that you have to have someone who is already a registered voter "vouch" — under oath and penalty of perjury — that you meet the qualifications to vote. In some counties, this person has to accompany you to the registrar's office; in others the voucher is interviewed later. Some counties limit the number of new applicants a registered voter can vouch for in a given year. Since no white voter would dare vouch for a Black applicant, in counties where only a handful of Blacks are registered only a few more can be added to the rolls each year even if they "pass" the so-called test. In counties where no Blacks are registered at all, none can register because no one will vouch for Black citizens hoping to vote.

Of course, any of these rules and requirements, including the so-called literacy test itself, can be ignored or altered at any time by whim of the Registrar. So most whites are not subject to this onerous process, and on occasion, a registrar might allow one or two Blacks to register in order to divert the attention of news reporters, or as a way of feigning compliance with some federal court order.

Your application and the results of your "literacy test" are reviewed by the three-member Board of Registrars — later in secret. They vote on whether you passed. It is entirely up to the judgment of the Board whether you passed or failed. Their judgment is final and cannot be appealed. Whites who miss every single question can still "pass" if — in the board's sole judgment — they are "qualified." If you are Black and get every question correct, they can still flunk you if, in their judgment, you are

The Selma Voting Righs Struggle

"unqualified" or of "poor moral character."

Your name is then published in a local newspaper listing of people who have applied to register. This is to make sure that all of your employers, landlords, mortgage-holders, business-suppliers, bank loan officers, and so on, are kept informed of this important event. All of the information on your application is quietly passed under the table to the White Citizens Council and Ku Klux Klan for appropriate action. Their role is to encourage you to withdraw your application — or withdraw yourself out of the county — by whatever means they deem necessary.

Today, people ask how anyone — white or Black — ever got through this mess to actually register? A good question. As a matter of public record, white registration in 1965 Alabama is very high, while Black registration is minuscule. In the counties where Afro-Americans are the majority of the population, white registration is often close to — or more than — 100%. In Lowndes County, for example, white registration stands at 118%. White registration can be more than 100% because the names of white voters who die or move out of the area are kept on the voting list. Oddly enough, many of them (even the dead ones), somehow manage to vote (for the incumbent) every election day. This is commonly referred to as the "tombstone vote." To the local politicians, it is a miracle of southern democracy.

In counties with large Black populations, however, Black voter registration ranges from under 10% to absolute zero— without a single Black voter in the entire county. In Lowndes and Wilcox counties, for example, some 70–80% of the people are Black but as of January 1965 when the Selma Voting Rights Campaign kicks off, none is registered to vote.

Alabama Voter Application

Today, most people register to vote by filling out a short form about the size of a postcard. In Alabama in 1965, the voter application form is four pages long.

A copy of the Alabama Voter Application form follows this

Literacy Tests for Voting Eligibility

section and is also at www.crmvet.org/info/litapp.pdf.

While the purpose of the first few questions on the application are obvious and similar to the questions asked of voter applicants today, other questions demand some explanation and background.

For example:

Race: The assumption is that people of mixed race are "Negro." If just one of your great-grandparents is Black, the Registrar considers you to be "Negro."

Are you a college student? If so, where? In 1965, colleges in the Deep South are still almost entirely segregated. The Black colleges are dependent on state governments (all white, of course) or white philanthropists for funding. When informed by the White Citizens Council that an Afro student has transgressed against the southern way of life by trying to register to vote, college presidents and deans are expected (required) to take disciplinary action or expel the student for the social crime of trying to vote.

List the places you have lived the past five years, giving town or county and state. Before statewide and national computerized police records, this data is used to locate arrest records you might have in other counties and states.

Are you employed? If so, state by whom. The White Citizens Council frequently informs employers when Black employees try to register. Immediate dismissal is expected. White employers who fail to fire such "troublemakers" can find themselves the target of a white business boycott or even Klan violence.

Have you ever been dishonorably discharged from military service? Bad conduct or dishonorable discharges are often used to deny registration to Black applicants though it is not clear what provision of Alabama laws justify that.

Have you ever been declared legally insane? Afro-Americans who resist the humiliations of segregation are sometimes declared "insane" and forcibly committed to institutions where they

The Selma Voting Rights Struggle

can be "cured" of their aberrant behavior. Once released, such persons can be legally barred from registering to vote by reason of insanity.

Give names and addresses of two persons who know you and can verify the statements made above by you relative to your residence in this state, county and precinct, ward or district. Whomever you list here can become a target of Citizen Council or Klan interest.

Have you ever seen a copy of this registration application form before receiving this copy today? The purpose of this question is to smoke out anyone who has attended a Freedom Movement voter-registration class. Such people are marked as "troublemakers" by the local power structure. (The voter application and sample questions shown on the web are from materials used in SCLC's Citizenship schools.)

Have you ever been convicted of any offense or paid any fine for violation of the law? Under Alabama law, most felons lose their right to vote either permanently or for some period depending on the type of crime. Registrars assume they have authority to deny the ballot to anyone who in their opinion is not of "good moral character." For Black applicants, even a misdemeanor conviction might be enough to show "bad" moral character. If you've never been arrested and sent to jail and therefore answer "No," but at some point in your life have paid a traffic ticket, a perjury charge could be made against you for "lying" on the form.

Oath: "answers are true" portion. Given the racist reality of the Alabama judicial system in 1965, this portion of the oath is — in effect — a form of intimidation. If you didn't answer all questions truthfully because of your legitimate fear of retaliation, or confusion over the question, then signing the oath places you at risk being charged with felony perjury as has happened to others in documented cases. Even if all of your answers are true, Alabama courts routinely convict Afro-Americans on blatantly false charges.

Oath: "affiliation" portion. In Alabama in 1965, the NAACP is an outlawed organization considered by the state to be

Literacy Tests for Voting Eligibility

"subversive." At various times, other civil rights organizations such as CORE, SNCC, and SCLC are all accused of being organizations that advocate the overthrow of the state. On occasion, Southern sheriffs and judges also construe nonviolent resistance to Jim Crow segregation laws as attempts to overthrow the state by unlawful means. So if you are a member of one of those organizations, or participated in anti-segregation protests, and you swear to this oath, you could — theoretically — be accused of perjury.

As a practical matter, by 1965 there is little chance of a Black applicant being charged or convicted of perjury for signing the registration oath. As late as 1960, such cases did still occur and for many applicants, the threat and intimidation linger.

What's missing from this form? It's hard to imagine that anything can be missing from a voter registration application that is four pages long — but something important *is* missing. If you examine the form carefully, you'll notice there is no way to state your party affiliation. You can't register as a Democrat, Republican, independent, or anything else. This omission is not an oversight; it is a deliberate tactic on the part of the white establishment to prevent Blacks from participating in the Democratic primary election as voters or candidates.

This is the era of the "solid South." Blacks are denied the right to vote and only white Democrats are elected. The white establishment, and most white voters, still hate Republicans as the "party of Lincoln" (today, some southern whites hate the Democrats as the "party of civil rights," although they don't admit it publicly). With Republican candidates un-electable, the vote that really matters is the Democratic primary. If there is no Republican or independent candidate (often the case in local elections), the winner of the Democratic primary simply assumes office. If there *is* a challenger from another party, the Democratic candidate always wins in the general election. Since there is no way to register as a Democrat, the party officials in each county get to determine who is a member of the party and therefore who is eligible to run for office and vote in the party primaries. They

The Selma Voting Righs Struggle

are determined to keep the primary for "whites only." This means that Blacks who somehow manage to become registered voters are still barred from the election that really counts.

Alabama Literacy Test

In addition to completing the application and swearing the oaths, you have to pass the so-called "literacy test" itself. Because the Freedom Movement is running Citizenship Schools to help people learn how to fill out the forms and pass the test, Alabama changes the test four times in 1964 and 1965. At the time of the Selma Voting Rights campaign, there are many different tests in use across the state.

A typical Alabama "literacy test" consists of parts "A," "B," and "C."

"Part A"

In Part "A" you are given a section of the Alabama Constitution to read aloud. The sections are taken from a big loose-leaf binder. Some are easier than others. If white applicants are given the test at all, they generally get the easy ones. The Registrar makes sure that Black applicants get the hardest ones — the ones filled with legalese and long convoluted sentences. For example, a white applicant might be given:

SECTION 20: That no person shall be imprisoned for debt.

While a Black applicant might be given:

SECTION 260: The income arising from the sixteenth section trust fund, the surplus revenue fund, until it is called for by the United States government, and the funds enumerated in sections 257 and 258 of this Constitution, together with a special annual tax of thirty cents on each one hundred dollars of taxable property in this state, which the legislature shall levy, shall be applied to the support and maintenance of the public schools, and it shall be the duty of the legislature to increase the

Literacy Tests for Voting Eligibility

public school fund from time to time as the necessity therefore and the condition of the treasury and the resources of the state may justify; provided, that nothing herein contained shall be so construed as to authorize the legislature to levy in any one year a greater rate of state taxation for all purposes, including schools, than sixty-five cents on each one hundred dollars' worth of taxable property; and provided further, that nothing herein contained shall prevent the legislature from first providing for the payment of the bonded indebtedness of the state and interest thereon out of all the revenue of the state.

The Registrar marks each word that *in his opinion* you mispronounce. In some counties, you have to orally interpret the section to the Registrar's satisfaction. You then have to either copy out by hand a section of the Constitution, or write it down from dictation as the Registrar mumbles it. White applicants usually are allowed to copy, while Black applicants usually have to take dictation. The Registrar then judges whether you are "literate" or "illiterate."

After that, you are given Parts "B" and "C" which are two sets of four written questions. You must answer all of them. For example:

"Part B"

1. Has the following part of the U.S. Constitution been changed? "Representatives shall be apportioned among the several states according to their respective numbers, counting the whole number of persons in each state, excluding Indians not taxed." _____

2. Which of the following is one of the duties of the United States Internal Revenue Service?

_____ passing legislation

_____ collection of income taxes

_____ giving welfare checks

3. There are three main types of city government in Alabama. Name one. _____

The Selma Voting Rights Struggle

4. Law requires that, "In God we trust" be placed on all money issues in the United States. _____

"Part C"

1. In what year did the Congress gain the right to prohibit the migration of persons to the states? _____

2. Who is the commander-in-chief of the army and navy of the United States? _____

3. Which of the parts above, of the United States Constitution, deals with the federal government's authority to call the state militia into federal service? _____

4. The president is forbidden to exercise his authority of pardon in cases of _____

Literacy Tests for Voting Eligibility

Photocopies of Alabama's literacy documents appear below and on the following pages. They are also archived online at www.crmvet.org/info/litques.pdf. These examples originated with the workbooks that Citizenship School teachers used to teach applicants what to expect when they went to an Alabama courthouse to register to vote.

APPLICATION FOR REGISTRATION, QUESTIONNAIRE AND OATHS

PART I

(This is to be filled in by a member of the Board of Registrars or a duly authorized clerk of the board. If applicant is a married woman, she must state given name by which she is known, maiden surname, and married surname, which shall be recorded as her full name.)

Full Name: _____
         Last   First   Middle

Date of Birth: _____ Sex _____ Race _____

Residence Address: _____

Mailing Address: _____

Voting Place: Precinct _____ Ward _____ District _____

Length of Residence: In State _____ County _____

Precinct, ward or district _____

Are you a member of the Armed Forces? _____

Are you the wife of a member of the Armed Forces? _____

Are you a college student? _____ If so, where _____

Have you ever been registered to vote in any other state or in any other county in Alabama? _____ If so, when and in what state and county and, if in Alabama, at what place did you vote in such county? _____

Highest grade, 1 to 12, completed _____ Where _____

Years college completed _____ Where _____

PART II

(To be filled in by the applicant in the presence of the Board of Registrars without assistance.)

I, _____, do hereby apply to the Board of Registrars of MONTGOMERY County, State of Alabama, to register as an elector under the Constitution and laws of the State of Alabama and do herewith submit my answers to the interrogatories propounded to me by the board.

_____
(Signature of Applicant)

1. Are you a citizen of the United States? _____
2. Where were you born? _____
3. If you are a naturalized citizen, give number appearing on your naturalization papers and date of issuance _____
4. Have you ever been married? _____ If so, give the name, residence and place of birth of your husband or wife _____

Are you divorced? _____

185

5. List the places you have lived the past five years, giving town or county and state.

6. Have you ever been known by any name other than the one appearing on this application?_____If so, state what name

7. Are you employed?_____If so, state by whom. (If you are self-employed, state this.)

8. Give the address of your present place of employment.

9. If, in the past five years, you have been employed by an employer other than your present employer, give name of all employers and cities and states in which you worked.

10. Has your name ever been stricken for any reason from any list of persons registered to vote?_____If so, where, when, and why?

11. Have you previously applied for and been denied registration as a voter?_____If so, when and where?

12. Have you ever served in the Armed Forces?_____If so, give dates, branch of service, and serial number

13. Have you ever been dishonorably discharged from military service?

14. Have you ever been declared legally insane?_____If so, give details

15. Give names and addresses of two persons who know you and can verify the statements made above by you relative to your residence in this state, county and precinct, ward or district.

16. Have you ever seen a copy of this registration application form before receiving this copy today?_____If so, when and where?

17. Have you ever been convicted of any offense or paid any fine for violation of the law?_____(Yes or No) If so, give the following information concerning each fine or conviction: charge, in what court tried, fine imposed, sentence, and, if paroled, state when, and if pardoned, state when. (If fine is for traffic violation only, you need write below only the words "traffic violation only.")

(Remainder of this form is to be filled out only as directed by an individual member of the Board of Registrars.)

PART III

Part III of this questionnaire shall consist of one of the forms which are Insert Part III as herein below set out. The insert shall be fastened to the questionnaire. The questions set out on the insert shall be answered according to the instructions therein set out. Each applicant shall demonstrate ability to read and write as required by the Constitution of Alabama, as amended, and no person shall be considered to have completed this application, nor shall the name of any applicant be entered upon the list of registered voters of any county until after such inserted Part III of the questionnaire has been satisfactorily completed and signed by the applicant.

Literacy Tests for Voting Eligibility

PLEASE INSERT PART III HERE

PART IV

OATHS

STATE OF ALABAMA

_____COUNTY

Before me,_____

a registrar in and for said county and state, personally appeared _____,

an applicant for registration as an elector, who being first duly sworn deposes and says:

"I do solemnly swear (or affirm) that the foregoing answers to the interrogatories are true and correct to the best of my knowledge, information and belief. I do further personally swear (or affirm) that I will support and defend the Constitution of the United States and the Constitution of the State of Alabama; that I do not believe in nor am I affiliated with any group or party which advocated or advocates the overthrow of the United States or the State of Alabama by unlawful means. I do further solemnly swear (or affirm) that in the matter of this application for registration I have spoken the truth, the whole truth and nothing but the truth, so help me God."

_____
(Signature of Applicant)

Sworn to and subscribed before me this the _____ day of _____, 19_____

_____
(Signature of Board Member)

EXPLANATION AND REMARKS

(Board members interviewing applicants may place here any special explanations, such as of residence status, or other remarks for purposes of clarification. If person is blind or is otherwise physically handicapped to such an extent that he cannot fill out this application form, the circumstances are to be recorded here, along with an explanation of the method used to determine if the person is, in fact, literate and can spell words and recognize those spelled to him, or can read large block letters and words in the case of persons with sight handicaps. _____

_____
_____

The Selma Voting Rights Struggle

PART V
ACTION OF THE BOARD

STATE OF ALABAMA
_____COUNTY

The applicant_____, appeared before the board of registrars for said state and county in a regular session and executed the foregoing application in the manner prescribed by law. The Board, having further examined said applicant under oath, touching his qualifications under Section 181, Constitution of Alabama, as amended, and having fully considered the foregoing application for registration, questionnaire and oaths, adjudges said applicant entitled to be registered and he was duly registered this the_____day of_____, 19___.

Signed:_____
Chairman

_____
Member

_____
Member

(NOTE: The act of actually determining an applicant entitled to be registered is judicial. A majority of the Board must concur. A majority must be present. The power cannot be delegated. Each member must vote on each application. Not until this is done may a certificate be issued the applicant.)

The Applicant,_____, due to failure to meet the requirements of state law for registration as an elector, is hereby rejected on this the_____day of_____, 19___.

Signed:_____
Chairman

_____
Member

_____
Member

PART VI
EXAMINATION OF SUPPORTING WITNESS

(The witness shall be placed under oath to tell the truth, the person administering the oath being a Board member or other person authorized to administer oaths and acting under the direction of the Board.)

Name of Witness_____

Address_____

Place of Voting_____

"I have known the applicant_____for_____years and_____months and I have personal knowledge that his place of residence is_____

and that he has resided in the State of Alabama at least one year and in_____County for at least six months."

_____
Signature of Witness

Sworn to and subscribed before me this the_____day of_____, 19___.

_____
(Person Administering Oath)

Date_____

Quotation Sources

1. *Ready for Revolution: The Life and Struggles of Stokely Carmichael*, Kwame Ture and Michael Thelwell.

2. *A Circle of Trust: Remembering SNCC*, Cheryl Lynn Greenberg

3. Interview: Jimmy Rogers and Linda Dehnad (www.crmvet.org)

4. Interview: Bruce Hartford (www.crmvet.org)

5. *SNCC: The New Abolitionists*, Howard Zinn.

6. *Bearing the Cross: Martin Luther King, & Southern Christian Leadership Conference*, David Garrow.

7. *Pillar of Fire, America in the King Years 1963-1965*, Taylor Branch.

8. *At Canaan's Edge—America in the King Years 1965-68*, Taylor Branch.

9. *Selma, Lord, Selma*, Sheyann Webb and Rachel West Nelson.

10. *Selma 1965: The March That Changed the South*, Charles Fager.

11. *Walking With the Wind*, John Lewis.

12. SNCC Report From Selma, Silas Norman and John Love (www.crmvet.org)

13. *Everybody Says Freedom: A History of the Civil Rights Movement in Songs and Pictures*, Pete Seeger & Bob Reiser.

14. Interview: Charles Bonner and Bettie Mae Fikes (www.crmvet.org).

15. *My Soul is Rested: The Story of the Civil Rights Movement in the Deep South*, Howell Raines.

16. Selma and the March to Montgomery: A Discussion (www.crmvet.org)

The Selma Voting Rights Struggle

17. *Hands on the Freedom Plow: Personal Accounts by Women in SNCC.*

18. "Insurgent Memories," Dr. Gwen Patton (www.crmvet.org)

19. *Sammy Younge, First Black College Student to Die in the Black Liberation Movement,* James Forman.

20. *The Good Doctors: The Medical Committee for Human Rights and the Struggle for Social Justice in Health Care,* John Dittmer.

21. *On the Road to Freedom: A Guided Tour of the Civil Rights Trail,* Charles Cobb.

22. *The Selma Campaign, 1963-1965: The Decisive Battle of the Civil Rights Movement,* Wally Vaughn and Hattie Campbell Davis, editors.

More information on the *Selma Freedom Movement and the March to Montgomery* is available on the Civil Rights Movement Veterans website www.crmvet.org.

About the Author

Bruce Hartford is the webspinner at the Civil Rights Movement Veterans website, www.crmvet.org. In 1963, he joined the Congress of Racial Equality (CORE) as a volunteer activist. In early 1965, he joined Dr. King's voting rights campaign in Selma, Alabama and participated in the March to Montgomery. As a field secretary for the Southern Christian Leadership Conference (SCLC), Bruce was project director for Crenshaw County voter registration. In the summer of 1966, he participated in the Meredith March Against Fear in Mississippi, and until 1967 was part of the SCLC field staff in Grenada, Mississippi during the long and bloody struggle to end segregation and win voter registration.

CPSIA information can be obtained at www.ICGtesting.com
Printed in the USA
BVOW05s0246090215
386935BV00001B/29/P